ᴬ Public Role
FOR THE
Private Sector

ᴬ Public Role
FOR THE
Private Sector

*Industry Self-Regulation
in a Global Economy*

Virginia Haufler

Carnegie Endowment for International Peace
WASHINGTON, D.C.

Carnegie Endowment for International Peace   Tel. 202-483-7600
1779 Massachusetts Avenue   Fax. 202-483-1840
Washington, D.C. 20036 USA   www.ceip.org

To order, contact Carnegie's distributor:
The Brookings Institution Press   Tel. 800-275-1447 or 202-797-6258
Department 029   Fax. 202-797-6004
Washington, D.C. 20042-0029 USA

The Carnegie Endowment for International Peace normally does not take institutional positions on public policy issues; the views presented in this publication are those of the individual authors and do not necessarily represent the views of the Carnegie Endowment, its officers, staff, or trustees.

Printed in the United States of America on acid-free, 85% recycled (30% post-consumer) paper with vegetable-oil based inks by Malloy Lithographing, Inc.

Interior design by Jenna Dixon. Text set in FB Wessex.

Library of Congress Cataloging-in-Publication Data

Haufler, Virginia, 1957-
    A public role for the private sector : industry self-regulation in a global economy /
Virginia Haufler
        p.   cm.
    Includes bibliographical references and index.
    ISBN 0-87003-176-7 (pbk. : alk. paper)
    1. Social responsibility of business. 2. Business ethics. 3. International business
enterprises—Moral and ethical aspects. 4. Corporations—Moral and ethical aspects.
5. International business enterprises—Social aspects. 6. International business
enterprises—Environmental aspects. 7. Globalization. 8. Labor laws and legislation.
9. Data protection—Law and legislation. 10. Foreign trade regulation. 11. Environmental law. I. Title.
HD60 .H392 2000
174'.4 – dc21   2001002352

07   06   05   04   03   02   01   5   4   3   2   1   1st Printing 2001

Contents

Foreword

MULTINATIONAL CORPORATIONS have taken advantage of increasingly integrated markets to organize production on a global scale. There now exist over 60,000 multinational corporations with more than 450,000 subsidiaries in every corner of the world. Major companies buy products from literally tens of thousands of subcontractors in developed and developing countries alike. The private sector is weaving together the world economy to an unprecedented degree.

In the process, most people believe that multinational corporations deliberately undermine national regulatory systems and drive standards down to the lowest common denominator. Yet, many companies participate in collective efforts to develop new international standards that go beyond what is required by national law. They develop technical standards that make international commerce easier to conduct. Increasingly, they also adopt policies that address urgent social issues. This evolving sense of social responsibility has not been taken seriously to date, yet it is a prominent feature of current corporate practice. Why would corporations voluntarily agree to adopt higher standards than legally required? In what areas are they most likely to do so? Can we view these practices as a form of regulation, and if so, how does it compete with traditional regulation? Is this just another illustration of the power of the private sector to shape world politics to its own ends? Or is this a new instrument for the resolution of pressing global problems?

A Public Role for the Private Sector: Industry Self-Regulation in a Global Economy provides a broad overview and analysis of recent changes in the role of the private sector in international affairs. It examines the contributions of the private sector to efforts to construct a new post–Cold War framework for the global political economy. This framework must accommodate rapid technological change, the integration of national markets into a global one, and the increasing transnationalism of political activism. This book explores such activities on three critical issues—environment, labor, and information privacy—to evaluate what drives changes in corporate behavior, and what effect these changes have on broader political and social conditions. This allows us to consider seriously the place of the private sector in providing governance to the world economy. The anwers raise significant concerns about the capacity of national governments to govern in a globalized economy. They also address important issues of accountability, legitimacy, and power if the private sector becomes a primary source for the development and implementation of rules, standards, and social norms.

It is impossible to understand contemporary transformations in world politics without understanding the role of the modern corporation, for it has become one of the most significant actors on the world scene. To this end, the Carnegie Endowment has established an ongoing project on the role of the private sector in international affairs. While on leave from the University of Maryland, Professor Virginia Haufler directed the first phase of this project. *The Public Role of the Private Sector* is a major contribution to a wider appreciation of the rapidly changing relationship between the public and private sectors in an era of great change.

JESSICA T. MATHEWS
President, Carnegie Endowment for International Peace

Preface

THIS BOOK STARTED as a small project to explore the public role of the private sector in setting international standards. When I began, I had no intention of getting mired in the debates over corporate social responsibility. Yet, as I began to collect material on international standard setting by the private sector I began to realize that almost every day the news would contain some tidbit about a new socially responsible corporate initiative. I became intrigued by the social and political implications of the changing role of business during a period of intense debate over the benefits and costs of globalization. It seemed that governments in the developed world were scaling back their social welfare programs but were torn over whether or not to demand that developing country trade partners reduce or expand their flimsy social programs. Political leaders of a variety of political persuasions began to look on corporate codes of conduct as a way to have their cake and eat it too: free trade but with someone else—multinational corporations—taking care of the side effects. Most of what had been written on this subject consisted of either single case studies that gave no real idea of the scope of what was happening, persuasive pieces designed to convince executives to jump on this new bandwagon, or critical essays condemning this as pure corporate public relations.

Support for this project came from the Carnegie Endowment for International Peace, under the leadership of Jessica Mathews. She recognized early on that the private sector had a public role to play, but that this raised all sorts of issues about power, governance, and accountability. I want to thank her for giving me the opportunity and support I needed to pursue this project.

I have to thank my associates at the Endowment for all their help: Ann Florini, Chantal de Jonge Oudraat, P. J. Simmons, William Drake, Marina Ottaway, Martha Olcott, and Tom Carothers. I would especially like to thank my assistant Michael Carriere, a Junior Fellow at the Carnegie Endowment, whose research assistance was invaluable. I also would like to thank the participants in the study group on the public role of the private sector and the panelists and attendees at the conference organized at the Carnegie Endowment. Thanks also go to all the people—too many to name individually—with whom I have discussed this project. They expressed sincere enthusiasm and were always helpful and insightful in discussions.

My hope is that this book will help readers understand the scope and character of an important element of the modern system of global governance. I hope it goes some way to finding a path between two different perspectives found in the literature and public debates over multinational corporations: the naive belief that corporate social responsibility can replace government authority versus the cynical stance that all corporate actions are corrupt. There are individuals both inside and outside the corporate community who are sincerely searching for the appropriate role for the private sector in the post–Cold War era.

Acronyms

AAMA	American Apparel Manufacturers Association
ACLU	American Civil Liberties Union
AFL-CIO	American Federation of Labor and the Congress of Industrial Organizations
AICPA	American Institute of Certified Public Accountants
AIP	Apparel Industry Partnership
APEC	Asia Pacific Economic Cooperation forum
BSR	Business for Social Responsibility
B2B	business to business
CEP	Council on Economic Priorities
CERES	Coalition for Environmentally Responsible Economies
CMA	Chemical Manufacturers Association
CNIL	Commission Nationale de l'Informatique et des Libertés
CPET	Canadian Partnership for Ethical Trading
ECOSOC	Economic and Social Council of the United Nations
EDF	Environmental Defense Fund
EMAS	European Union Eco-Management and Audit Scheme
EMS	environmental management system
EPIC	Electronic Privacy Information Center
ETAG	Ethical Trading Action Group
ETI	Ethical Trading Initiative
EU	European Union
FAO	Food and Agriculture Organization
FLA	Fair Labor Association
FSC	Forest Stewardship Council
GATT	General Agreement on Tariffs and Trade
GEMI	Global Environmental Management Initiative
GRI	Global Reporting Initiative
ICC	International Chamber of Commerce
ICCA	International Council of Chemical Associations

ICCR	Interfaith Center on Corporate Responsibility
ICFTU	International Confederation of Free Trade Unions
ILO	International Labor Organization
IMF	International Monetary Fund
IRRC	Investor Responsibility Research Center
ISO	International Organization for Standardization
ITT	International Telephone and Telegraph
MAI	Multilateral Agreement on Investment
MNC	Multinational corporation
NAFTA	North American Free Trade Agreement
NGO	nongovernmental organization
OECD	Organization for Economic Cooperation and Development
OPA	Online Privacy Alliance
OPEC	Organization of Petroleum Exporting Countries
PERI	Public Environmental Reporting Initiative
PWBLF	Prince of Wales Business Leaders Forum
P3P	Platform for Privacy Preferences
SAI	Social Accountability International
SRI	socially responsible investment
TACD	Trans-Atlantic Consumer Dialogue
TNC	transnational corporation
UNCED	UN Conference on Environment and Development
UNDP	UN Development Program
UNEP	UN Environment Program
UNCTAD	UN Conference on Trade and Development
UNICEF	UN Children's Fund
UNITE	Union of Needletrades, Industrial, and Textile Employees
WBCSD	World Business Council for Sustainable Development
WHO	World Health Organization
WRAP	Worldwide Responsible Apparel Production Principles and Certification Program
WTO	World Trade Organization

Introduction

IN THE PAST DECADE, most major multinational corporations (MNCs) —and many smaller ones—have rushed to develop new codes of conduct that set standards for their behavior on issues that top the international agenda. These issues include everything from the use of sweatshop labor to the level of carbon emissions from their factories. In a turnabout from the past, many companies now actively seek out their critics in the nonprofit world as partners for new social and environmental programs. Some dismiss this new approach as a public relations ploy designed to ward off government regulation and make the companies look good to consumers. Proponents argue that these voluntary standards have a significant positive influence on the behavior of companies and are more flexible and easier to implement than traditional industry regulation. All sides view industry self-regulation as a potential new source of *global governance*, that is, mechanisms to reach collective decisions about transnational problems with or without government participation. What they do not agree on is whether this is a legitimate and effective means to achieve public policy goals.

Globalization has made the regulation of MNCs one of the most contentious issues in relations among states and within societies. Competing states have not been able to negotiate comprehensive rules regarding corporate rights and responsibilities, as demonstrated by the failure of the recent negotiations over a Multilateral Agreement on Investment (MAI).[1] At the national level, most industrialized and many developing countries are moving toward a more market friendly system of regulation, in which governments often delegate numerous responsibilities to the private sector (Aman 1999). Businesses are being pushed and pulled to adopt voluntary standards by their fear of ill-conceived international rules and transnational activist pressure, of heightened competition in a world in which reputation matters, and of the spread of new ideas within the business world about how to achieve long-term profitable growth. Governments are interested in legitimizing these efforts in the hope that they can protect society from the negative side effects of corporate activities in a flexible way that maintains national competitiveness.

The problem that governments and publics have with these voluntary initiatives is precisely that they are voluntary, with often-weak enforcement mechanisms. Few people trust business to implement higher standards and stick by them. This is further complicated by the fact that most of these initiatives are fundamentally about the activities of a corporation *in other countries*. Governments and publics in the industrialized countries, in which regulatory systems are strong and well developed, want the private sector to raise standards in developing countries. Many critics fear that the ability of international investors to move easily from country to country will lead to a "race to the bottom" as companies seek out sources of low-cost production, which often means countries with weak regulatory systems.[2] Industry self-regulation may be one way to raise standards, but because those standards are voluntary and unenforceable, they lack credibility. Even more troubling for many, however, is the issue of accountability. If these efforts are an indirect means for public goals to be met by private interests, then how does the public influence their content? How can the public make sure the private sector upholds its end of this one-sided bargain? Without the public having a voice, these new forms of regulation appear to be undemocratic and illegitimate.

This book addresses three overarching questions raised by the trend of industry self-regulation. First, why would industry go beyond what is required by national and international regulation and put significant constraints on its own behavior? Second, how do the participants in self-regulation deal with issues of enforcement, accountability, transparency, and credibility? Third, how should governments and publics view these industry activities?

To answer these questions, this book begins with an overview of the current state of play in industry self-regulation and the context in which it is developing. The discussion in subsequent chapters then moves to three policy arenas in which debates over industry self-regulation are most prominent: environment, labor, and privacy. These are all cases in which one of the main points of contention is the behavior of business in global markets. All three areas raise questions about how multinational corporations should handle overseas production and exchange relations. Under what conditions would we expect to see more industry self-regulation? As will be demonstrated in the following chapters, the most potent confluence of factors is a high risk of government regulation at the national or international level; relatively low economic competition but high asset specificity; high probability of transnational activist pressure; reputation as a key asset of the company or industry involved; and high levels of information exchange, learning, and consensus within the industry. This particular confluence is rare, and the three cases are each quite different in this regard. Yet, in every case, industry self-regulation has become a key element of the policy debate.

Given these expectations about the conditions that lead companies to choose to self-regulate, the next step is to explore exactly how they do it and what concerns are raised by their initiatives. There is a surprising variety of programs: from corporate codes to monitoring systems to elaborate partnerships with nongovernmental organizations (NGOs) or governments in a form of co-regulation. Many of these programs seek to assure some sort of credibility and accountability for the voluntary initiatives, and use what might be called "soft enforcement," that is, reputation and transparency to leverage public pressure to ensure the commitments made by the firm are upheld.

The three case studies explore the factors that appear to drive firms toward self-regulation, the variety of commitments those firms undertake, and the tensions that arise between public and private interests. Each chapter examines codes adopted by individual firms; those adopted through industrywide negotiation; and those either developed through a partnership among business and other entities, or developed by NGOs, intergovernmental organizations, and states and presented to the private sector for adoption. Each chapter describes the systems of management implementation, monitoring, and transparency being developed. Finally, each explores the degree to which these voluntary programs might meet public expectations. The data for these cases were current as of March 2001; these are dynamic arenas, though, where continued change is inevitable.

Voluntary standard setting by firms is a logical response to the ambiguities and uncertainties of the current global system. It responds to societal pressure, while avoiding rigid government interference. It is voluntary and therefore can be applied in a flexible manner. It is potentially global in scope, and if adopted widely, would reduce costs, increase efficiency, and prevent other corporations from gaining competitive advantage. Governments seeking to find some way to provide social protections to the public—at home and abroad—while strengthening national economic competitiveness look on corporate social responsibility as an element of the "third way" between socialism and capitalism.[3] Political interests on the left and right are becoming more interested in exploring and supporting corporate voluntary initiatives to deal with the backlash against globalization and to maintain open markets. Private sector self-regulation appears to its supporters as a way to balance the interests of business and society without expanding government intervention in the economy.

Nevertheless, three questions arise repeatedly in evaluating these efforts: How are these voluntary measures enforced, if at all? How credible are business commitments, given the lack of strong enforcement? And how accountable is business to the wider public when adopting these nondemocratic standards? Harrison, in a review of purely national programs in the United States and Canada, comes to mixed conclusions about the effectiveness of corporate environmental self-regulation (Harrison 1999). Gordon, however, argues in a recent paper that nonbinding agreements (such as industry self-regulatory commitments) have an important role to play in experimenting with new rules and creating consensus for eventual public regulation (Gordon 1999; see also Chayes and Chayes 1998).

If the kind of standard-setting activity represented in these three cases becomes widespread, then it will present new challenges for all the participants. The concluding chapter in this book addresses self-regulation in light of arguments about corporate power and discusses the challenge that such corporate action presents to governments and NGOs. It also presents a broader view of the results of industry self-regulation and what it means for global governance.

Governments will have to consider how industry self-regulation affects domestic regulatory capacity, because it can compete with or supplement national regulatory norms, even though applied to industry activities abroad. On the one hand, relying on voluntary initiatives certainly lowers the cost of influencing and monitoring business behavior. In fact, the existence of such initiatives challenges governments to develop new institutional incentives for the private sector to expand these activities. On the other hand, these initiatives probably will not relieve the pressure on governments to intervene, because in many cases the implementation of these codes is weak. Nevertheless, the industrialized countries may view these voluntary private sector initiatives as a way to resolve the tensions between promoting both foreign investment and high standards at the same time. Some may argue that these initiatives simply reflect the decreasing capacity of these governments to regulate domestically or to negotiate international agreements about the behavior of MNCs.[4] The international integration of markets has changed the ability and willingness of states to intervene in economic affairs, or at least, in the affairs of MNCs. These initiatives could ultimately increase the backlash against globalization, if they appear to be an abdication to the private sector of government responsibility.

Private sector standard setting also poses new challenges for NGOs. To the degree that voluntary initiatives actually raise standards, the business sector will expect less criticism from these groups. NGOs will need to publicize good behavior, instead of concentrating all their attention on the bad. But the level of trust between many NGOs and the business community is quite low, and many activists simply do not accept the legitimacy of the corporate community on any level. Some organizations may be willing to engage in dialogue and form partnerships with business for specific projects, but they may not be able to sustain a long-term relationship. Because the standards embodied in corporate initiatives will never meet the criteria of all the diverse groups watching the private sector, and because implementation systems are weak, the perceived failures of these exercises will tempt many NGOs to turn their backs on industry and concentrate on highlighting the violations of business and lobbying for strict regulation.

Richard Newton, director of BP Europe, noted recently: "If people *think* you have power, then—to some degree at least—you do" (Buchan 1998). Both the perception and reality of corporate power in a global economy have made the role of the private sector in international affairs a source of constant contention. The shift in power away from governments portends a future in which the relationship between business and society may be very different from what we see today.

I

Public and Private Interests in Global Regulation: An Overview of the Issues

THE PUBLIC AND MOST POLITICIANS are just beginning to engage in serious debate over the conditions under which industry self-regulation makes sense in the era of globalization. This debate requires more understanding of the driving forces behind this trend—forces that reflect the relative power of governments to rule, industry to gain authority in new spheres, and the public to influence policy. Many people have decried the effects of globalization and argue that power is shifting dramatically into the hands of corporations. William Greider titled his recent book *One World, Ready or Not*; David Korten called his book *When Corporations Rule the World* (Greider 1997; Korten 1995). The examples they give present a picture of politicians bowing to the demands of big business, often in a corrupt way.[5] Internationally, corporations are accused of skipping lightly from country to country in search of the most accommodating political environment. But if this is true, then any efforts by MNCs to restrain their own behavior—however weak those restraints may be—must be considered an anomaly. Why do it?

To begin to answer this fundamental question, this chapter first defines self-regulation and its elements and then examines the context in which industry self-regulation is taking place. The next section turns to the issue of how globalization is changing the character of business, forcing it to take on new roles in the public domain. It then offers a brief survey of international regulatory efforts to date. Finally, it identifies and explores the factors that are driving industry to self-regulation.

The Context for Industry Self-Regulation

Technically, regulation is action or behavior that is required by governments—it is not voluntary, and the regulators are public authorities.[6] But in broader, more practical terms, regulation is the formal rules or standards that dictate what is acceptable and required behavior, putting limits on what is permissible.[7] Self-regulation occurs when those regulated—in this case, corporations—design and enforce the rules themselves. The rules that govern their behavior are adopted voluntarily, either going beyond current regulatory requirements or establishing new standards in areas in which government rules or standards are lacking. Although they are adopted voluntarily, the rules may be backed up with a variety of formal and informal enforcement mechanisms including written agreements among companies or between companies and other groups. The basic document of such an initiative typically is a "corporate code of conduct." A recent description of the nature of agreements between states could just as well apply to corporate codes, especially when they involve more than one firm:

> The agreements vary widely in scope, number of parties, and degree of specificity, as well as in subject matter. Some are little more than statements of principle or agreements to agree. Others contain detailed prescriptions for behavior in a defined field. Still others may be umbrella agreements for consensus building in preparation for more specific regulation later. Often they create international organizations to oversee the enterprise. (Chayes and Chayes 1998, 1)

Two types of industry standard setting are often held up as models for business self-regulation, and they influence the character of the trends we see today. First, from a business perspective, the way to develop international standards is the way they have always been developed for technical advances or market promotion. These standards specify the physical qualities required for the sale and use of industrial or commercial products and services, or the terms under which business exchanges will occur. Industry associations have a long history of designing and promoting good design practices for their members and have taken the initiative to develop new standards for emerging technologies. These are intended to facilitate international exchange of goods and services, enhance the reputation of the industry as a whole, and reduce the costs of doing business. For instance, the pharmaceutical industry has strict standards for marketing drugs, because bad practices will undermine consumer trust and potentially weaken the market. International bodies such as the International Organization for Standardization (ISO), whose members are a mix of government and nongovernment representatives, negotiate agreements that specify the rules, guidelines, and characteristics for materials, products, processes, and services. For some forms of contemporary self-regulatory activity, this technical model dominates industry thinking.

The second model comes from the activist initiatives of the 1970s and 1980s and is much more foreign to the business mind. This model is based on social or political demands from outside the business community. The Sullivan and MacBride Principles, for apartheid South Africa and conflict-ridden Northern Ireland, respectively, are two early examples. Despite their mixed record, both efforts brought to the attention of a wide audience the possibilities for achieving social reform through a change in corporate behavior. They thus set the stage for the next phase in corporate regulation. That next phase is what we are seeing now, a "corporate accountability" movement in which civil society groups pressure companies to develop codes of conduct or to adopt commitments developed by others (Broad and Cavanagh 1998). In many cases, a crisis such as an oil spill or the exposure of sweatshop conditions in a factory triggers the mobilization of pressure groups and leads to the development of new industry principles. For instance, the *Exxon Valdez* oil spill eventually led a small group of environmentalists and sympathetic business executives to develop and adopt the Coalition for Environmentally Responsible Economies (CERES) Principles on environmental responsibility. In this case, industry developed standards not to address technical concerns or make it easier to exchange goods and services, but rather in response to social demands.

The trend toward self-regulation went relatively unnoticed until recently. This may be in part because the phenomenon itself is difficult to see. We tend to assume that regulation is an activity of governments, therefore blinding ourselves to other varieties of rule. Much self-regulation occurs as a matter of course within industry associations and is viewed as simply a process of determining business "best practices" or as something that leads to obscure technical standards.[8] Corporations increasingly have begun to adopt codes of conduct that lay out their rights and responsibilities, but they have done so in such an ad hoc fashion that it is difficult to determine the scope of the codes. Only recently have different projects begun to collect and analyze corporate codes. Social and political partnerships among corporations, international organizations, governments, and nongovernmental actors have expanded in number, but their purpose is often such a mix of providing public goods and services, setting industry standards, and obtaining private benefits that their regulatory aspect is hard to see.

The main participants in self-regulation are MNCs based in the industrialized countries.[9] Changes in the international system provide them with increasing access to a large number of markets hitherto closed to them. The most dramatic opportunity is China's entry into the World Trade Organization (WTO) portending a great reorganization of the world economy. Both large and small firms have an international presence through trade, joint ventures, strategic alliances, outsourcing of production to local manufacturers abroad, and in recent years, via the Internet (Oman 1984; Gomes-Casseres 1994).[10] Intense competition for markets pushes all firms to produce at lower cost, with higher quality, and to respond to changing consumer demands almost instantaneously. In their operations in developing countries, firms face myriad conflicting cultures, often-weak national governments, and markets so thin of economic activity that foreign corporations easily dominate them. They also find themselves dealing with a tangle of law and regulation at multiple levels of government on a variety of policy issues. Many corporations that invest and transact business internationally are torn between a desire for harmonization and standardization of the rules of the game, and strategic calculations about the competitive edge that they could gain from taking advantage of such a mixed system.[11]

Corporate leaders consistently express anxiety at the thought of government intervention, especially in the most competitive sectors. This concern exists even though deregulation, privatization, and market-oriented policies have become widely accepted around the world in the past two decades. Governments increasingly view their own roles as that of facilitators of market expansion and competitiveness.[12] Politicians of both the left and right advocate smaller government and more market-friendly regulation, including delegation of tasks to the private sector.[13] Former U.S. president Bill Clinton famously declared that "the era of big government is dead."

Despite this overall liberalizing trend, we now see the public in many countries demanding that government deal with the downside of globalization.[14] Riots in Seattle over the WTO, protests in Washington, D.C., over World Bank and International Monetary Fund (IMF) policies, and activist mobilization for any major international economic gathering reflect a growing uneasiness with the economic forces unleashed in the past few decades. Those forces are embodied in the MNC. In a May 1999 poll in Great Britain, over 50 percent of those surveyed disagreed with the statement that the profits of large companies make things better for everyone who uses their products and services—a percentage that had steadily increased over the past decade (MORI 1999).

The demands of consumers, activists, and the media—which are all active transnationally—are expanding. Nongovernmental advocacy organizations in particular have become more effective in constructing transnational issue networks to press their causes in many different political arenas at once (Florini 2000; Mathews 1997; Keck and Sikkink 1998; Simmons 1998). For some issues, activists who are blocked in their efforts to persuade governments to regulate and punish corporate transgressors now target the business community directly (Broad and Cavanagh 1998). They use the media to expose corporate violators, protest against a company, bring lawsuits against specific companies or industries, and generally raise the costs—economically and politically—of doing business.[15] They mobilize consumers and investors as a strategy to effect corporate change. Consumers demand high quality and low cost in the products and services they buy, but they also increasingly expect business to produce them in ways that do not have negative consequences for society. Investors also pressure corporate leaders by investing in socially responsible companies and bringing shareholder resolutions to annual meetings. Shareholder activism is increasing in the United States and Europe, and to some degree the "shareholder" perspective on corporate governance is giving way to "stakeholder" perspectives.[16] This is the context in which businesses are turning toward self-regulatory strategies.

Globalization and Changes in the Character of Business

Industry self-regulation is one element of globalization. Continuous debate about the causes and consequences of globalization has yet to lead to any consensus about the nature of the phenomenon. The core of the debate, however, can be summed up by the term *convergence.* Some people debate whether global economic integration forces all governments to adopt similar policies, such as free trade or loosened restrictions on foreign investment (Berger and Dore 1996; Boyer and Drache 1996; Prakash and Hart 1999). Others argue over whether globalization forces political parties to adopt similar platforms, and whether there is a convergence in partisan politics (Garrett 1998). Many point to the decline in state power as a hallmark of globalization, affecting all countries, even the most powerful (Hirst and Thompson 1995; Ohmae 1995; Strange 1996; Mathews 1997). A small number of scholars have tried to assess whether global economic pressures lead to convergence in the organization and market behavior of firms (Doremus et al. 1998). Even fewer address systematically whether globalization leads to convergence in the political roles adopted by firms, and how this might affect the relationship between the public and private sectors in governing the world economy.

This project starts from the empirical observation that many MNCs are adopting a variety of self-regulatory policies and are doing so at an increasing rate. Self-regulatory policies include: corporate codes of conduct that lay out the social commitments the company makes; management and accounting systems that translate those commitments into specific roles and responsibilities within the organization; implementation programs that involve the expenditure of resources to achieve specific goals; and monitoring, auditing, certification, and labeling programs that testify to successful achievement. Industry self-regulation also shades into "co-regulation" at times, when the policies and programs are developed in cooperation with governments. Much of this activity falls under the more popular headings of corporate social responsibility, corporate citizenship, and business ethics.

The Organization for Economic Cooperation and Development (OECD) recently analyzed a sample of 233 corporate codes of conduct.

This analysis demonstrated that a growing number of companies either adopted or revised their codes of conduct in the past decade (OECD 1998). In a recent survey, KPMG reported that of 1,000 large Canadian companies 86.4 percent have codes stating their values and principles, and 72.7 percent conduct programs focusing on promoting ethical values and practices (KPMG 2000). A recent International Labor Organization (ILO) report on voluntary initiatives found the same upward trend in the number of codes addressing labor issues. Indirectly, corporate interest can be gauged by the increasingly large audience for the annual meetings of Business for Social Responsibility (BSR), a U.S.-based business membership organization. The Prince of Wales Business Leaders Forum (PWBLF) in the United Kingdom, made up of British firms, has gained more and more visibility and influence in promoting corporate social responsibility. The Sullivan Principles, originally developed for companies in apartheid South Africa, have been revised to become general global guidelines, and many companies are signing up. The UN Global Compact, under which corporations commit to uphold nine principles drawn from UN agreements, is beginning to attract major MNCs. Membership in the U.S.-based Association of Ethics Officers went from only twelve in 1993 to over 700 today, as more firms feel the need to have ethics and compliance officers (Ethics Officers Association 2000).[17] The number of business conferences devoted to business ethics, corporate social responsibility, codes of conduct, and related topics has mushroomed (although no exact figures are available). Even the U.S. Chamber of Commerce—not usually viewed as a progressive organization—recently established a Corporate Citizenship Center.

Corporate codes of conduct are generally the most visible measure of industry self-regulation. However, there is now an array of other elements in this emerging self-regulatory system. An increasing number of management programs support the implementation of conduct codes within the corporate bureaucracy. These internal management systems include auditing, accounting, monitoring, and reporting requirements. In fact, there has been such a proliferation in environmental reporting alone that the UN Environment Program (UNEP), in partnership with business organizations and NGOs, has convened a Global Reporting Initiative (GRI) in an effort to standardize and make sense of the competing formats. Hundreds of international firms have adopted environmental management systems, including the ISO 14000 standards, which require companies to develop links between a corporate environmental code and actual implementation throughout the organization.[18] Monitoring and auditing of performance have become so common that the major auditing and accounting firms now have well-established practices in this new market, with PricewaterhouseCoopers taking an early lead in the market for social audits of factories. Businesses have created new associations to develop and implement standards, often partnering with NGOs, for example, in the Fair Labor Association for apparel manufacturers in the United States. Many companies have moved from simple codes of conduct developed by top management to bottom-up policy processes within the entire company. Still others have moved from codes developed in-house to collective efforts within an industry or business group. Others have developed more elaborate systems that institutionalize new practices and certify their implementation. For example, Mattel has established an independent monitoring organization that publishes its report on practices in overseas suppliers' factories.

What is particularly noteworthy about the current trend, however, is the degree to which the private sector is pursuing self-regulatory actions in areas that are typically *not* viewed as essential to their core economic activities. Voluntary codes and standards do not address narrow technical issues alone. They also do not entirely fit under the heading of traditional philanthropic programs, although some corporate executives think of them this way. They address what might be called the externalities of corporate activity—the side effects of modern production, distribution, sales, and service. The existence of these externalities is often given as the justification for government intervention to correct this "market failure." To date, however, governments have not been very effective at intervening at the international level to regulate corporate behavior on social and environmental issues.

How should we view these developments? Do they signify a new trend in how corporations behave and what expectations society has of them? Or are they simply an effort to distract attention from an underlying disconnect between the interests of the private sector and those of the public?

A Survey of International Regulation of Multinational Corporations

The regulation of private sector activity historically has traded back and forth between public and private hands. Industry self-regulation, especially for cross-border exchanges, is not an entirely new phenomenon, but it periodically falls out of favor. During the sixteenth century, when long-distance trade became common throughout Europe, merchants developed their own system of rules for exchanging money and goods and for settling disputes that were independent of political jurisdiction (Braudel 1981–1984). Over the course of the next few centuries, as political leaders consolidated the new sovereign nation-states in Europe, they often adopted and codified this merchant law, gradually drawing a line between private activity and public rule making. By the mid-twentieth century, the area of private rule making gave way to an expansion of the public sector in many dimensions. Only in the past twenty years has the separation between the public and private sectors become less rigid, as state intervention in economic affairs has been reversed by a wave of privatization and deregulation. Much of the new private sector governance responds to gaps in global governance that stem from the lack of overarching, comprehensive regulation of corporations at the international level.

Governments have repeatedly tried in the past few decades to develop an effective regime for regulating international corporate behavior but have never successfully negotiated a strong and comprehensive system. Since MNCs first emerged as a significant force after World War II, regulation of them has generally been by individual countries and not by international law and organizations, although this issue has certainly been on the agenda during the entire post-World War II era. The effort to use international law to regulate corporations reached a high point in the 1970s, when the United Nations sponsored negotiations over a proposed voluntary Code of Conduct on Transnational Corporations, the OECD developed its Guidelines for Multinational Enterprises, and the ILO adopted its tripartite Declaration of Principles Concerning Multinational Enterprises and Social Policy. Governments also negotiated sectoral agreements as a result of contentious debates over specific industry practices, such as the marketing of infant formula in developing countries. In Latin America, countries responded to the entry of foreign investors with the creation of a set of regional investment codes (Lipson 1985).[19] Both developing nations and trade unions in the 1970s agreed that the power of international business needed to be reined in as part of a New International Economic Order, but their efforts failed (Kline 1985).

The climate of the early 1970s played an important role in capturing the collective attention of the United Nations and others on the issue of corporate behavior. Corporate influence on national politics had become a pressing concern, particularly in newly independent states still uncertain of their sovereignty. Scandals had erupted, for instance, over the role of the International Telephone and Telegraph company (ITT) in Chile. In response to developing country demands, the Economic and Social Council of the United Nations (ECOSOC) in 1972 adopted a resolution to monitor closely the behavior of transnational corporations (TNCs). ECOSOC established the Commission on Transnational Corporations in 1974 with the mandate to negotiate a code of conduct for TNCs. Under the proposed UN Code, states would pledge to ensure that foreign investors respected national sovereignty and human rights, disclosed relevant information to host governments about their operations, refrained from transfer pricing, and resolved other points of contention.[20] From the very start, the United Nations assumed the end result would be a comprehensive, single international instrument.

Developing countries, empowered by the success of the Organization of Petroleum Exporting Countries (OPEC) oil embargo in 1972, insisted that the industrialized world make the code mandatory and apply it only to TNCs and not to the governments that host them. The major industrialized nations, however, supported a voluntary code that addressed both host government and corporate behavior. In the early negotiations, the issues of nationalization and compensation of foreign corporate assets and the national treatment of foreign companies tied up the discussions. The UN debate over a corporate code became a flash point for conflicts between the developing and industrialized countries, exacerbated by Cold War tensions and the ideological fight between capitalism and communism. The negotiations dragged on throughout the decade.

By 1985, efforts to develop an international corporate code had stagnated (Kline 1985). In both the United States and the United Kingdom the political wind had turned by the 1980s, and new governments ardently pursued free market policies that went against further regulation of corporations. Many developing countries were suffering through a debt crisis and under the guidance of the IMF adopted deregulatory policies themselves. They were no longer very interested in the UN Code negotiations. In 1991, the Bush administration argued that private corporations played a critical role in the world economy and therefore should not be regulated. In 1992, despite agreement on about 80 percent of the content of the code, the international negotiations ended.[21]

Simultaneously with the UN negotiations, the OECD managed to negotiate and adopt Guidelines for Multinational Enterprises in 1976 as part of a broader Declaration on International Investment and Multinational Enterprises. The member states—the industrialized nations—negotiated principles that governments would apply voluntarily to the private sector. The guidelines covered issues from financing and taxation to employment and environmental protection. They had little influence and visibility, however, despite the fact that the OECD revised them twice in the following decades.

A year after the initial guidelines were adopted by the OECD, the ILO also formulated and adopted a Declaration of Principles Concerning Multinational Enterprises and Social Policy. The declaration established voluntary guidelines covering employment, training, working conditions, and industrial relations. As in all ILO conventions, the declaration applied to governments and relied on them to ratify and implement its provisions. The ILO instrument places more restrictions on MNC activity than the OECD document but is not as comprehensive as the UN Code would have been. Both the OECD Guidelines and the ILO Declaration did not have much direct and measurable effect, but they laid the groundwork for later efforts.

The concern over multinational corporate behavior did not pass with the formulation and adoption of the OECD Guidelines or the ILO Declaration. Although interest in developing a multilateral code of conduct waned in the 1980s, specific issues did grab the headlines. The most significant was the movement to use corporations as levers to change the apartheid regime in South Africa. In 1977, the Reverend Leon Sullivan, a member of the Board of General Motors and an activist against apartheid, developed a set of principles to guide companies operating in South Africa, hoping the private sector could change the system from within. By 1984, 128 of about 350 U.S. companies operating in South Africa had agreed to abide by these principles. Despite this affirmation by so many U.S. companies, Sullivan himself began to lose faith in the efficacy of the principles because too many companies did not implement them and because the apartheid regime appeared so firmly entrenched. He began to advocate divestment from South Africa, as many others did. Yet, in hindsight, the Sullivan Principles were an important piece in the ultimately successful movement against apartheid. Both the Sullivan Principles and the divestment movement demonstrated the potential of using corporations as tools to pursue political objectives (Klotz 1995).[22]

In the past decade, smaller groups of states have been able to negotiate and implement rules governing corporate behavior. These regional regulations are fairly comprehensive, covering both corporate rights and responsibilities. The two major advances in this area are the Social Protocol of the European Union (EU) and the labor and environment side agreements of the North American Free Trade Agreement (NAFTA). These two agreements, despite significant weaknesses, establish wider acceptance of the idea that corporations must be held to high standards. Some EU member states disagree on whether labor and environmental standards should be harmonized and have opted out of the Social Protocol (there is much less disagreement, however, over the strong human rights protections in EU law). The NAFTA side agreements adopted in 1993 specifically addressed some of the social and environmental side effects of cross-border investment within North America. The main treaty, enforceable under international law, covers property rights and national treatment for foreign investors. The NAFTA side agreements and the institutions established to monitor them have no authority over domestic regulatory systems but essentially commit member governments to live up to their own current law and regulation. Both the EU Social Protocol and the NAFTA side agreements apply to what some might call the "easy" cases—multinational corporate behavior in relatively advanced, industrialized countries, with high standards already written into law. Most of the big problems with multinationals occur in the developing world.

In the 1990s, as the backlash against globalization and corporate power gained strength, the OECD launched two new efforts: one, to revise the existing Guidelines for Multinational Enterprises, and two, to sponsor negotiations over a comprehensive and enforceable MAI. The MAI would lay out such principles as national treatment for foreign investment, protection of property rights, and arbitration requirements. It was a complicated document full of trade-offs to protect the interests of different industries and countries, and it garnered only weak support among the member governments. The United States alone had approximately 500 pages of reservations to the proposed treaty. A loose coalition of environmental, human rights, and anticorporate organizations put the final nail in the coffin of the proposed MAI by mobilizing energetically against an agreement that they argued protected the rights of corporations without paying equivalent attention to their responsibilities.[23]

In contrast, the OECD successfully concluded another revision of the original Guidelines for Multinational Enterprises in June 2000, strengthening its provisions significantly. The new OECD Guidelines have wider acceptance, with some non-OECD newly industrializing countries such as South Korea and Brazil indicating a desire to adopt them. These guidelines will be monitored through national contact points in each country (Aaronson 2000). It is too early to tell whether they will eventually become a strong instrument of corporate regulation, but the history of earlier efforts leads one to doubt it.

This brief survey of international regulatory efforts demonstrates the waxing and waning of interest in them in the past three decades. The UN, ILO, and OECD all attempted to develop comprehensive frameworks for corporate behavior, but these early initiatives had little impact. In recent years, all three organizations have revitalized their attention to corporate activities. At the same time, however, the private sector has not remained immune to the pressures of their changing social environment. The public's expectations regarding corporate behavior have changed, and many companies are responding to these changes with their own principles, guidelines, practices, and codes.

Factors Driving Industry Self-Regulation: Risk, Reputation, and Learning

What factors are driving the private sector to step forward with proposals to put limits on their own behavior? Even if those limits are not very constraining or only weakly enforced, why do they even feel compelled to talk about this now? We can identify three major factors that influence corporate decision making in this area: risk, reputation, and learning. Self-regulatory strategies are chosen to reduce risk, enhance reputation, and respond to new ideas within the business community.

Risk: Political and Economic Challenges and Uncertainties

The idea that business strategy is influenced by assessments of risk is not a new one. Economists and business scholars have been analyzing risk in corporate decision making for a long time. They examine the risks involved in launching new products, entering new markets, and reacting to the competitive strategies of other firms. In the past few decades, a number of scholars have also begun to explore the influence of political risk on decisions and outcomes. Political risk includes the probability that a corporation setting up operations in a foreign country might face the threat of expropriation, nationalization, war, or profound changes in the legal environment.[24] The more dramatic threats usually make corporate executives reconsider their decision to invest in a country or may encourage them to leave. The problems addressed by self-regulation arise when a company decides to go in and stay, despite potential political risks.

The risk of loss due to violence from war, civil war, riot, rebellion, and terrorism can be one of the most difficult challenges facing any business. Such risk entails destruction of property, shutting down of business operations, and direct harm to corporate personnel. In Nigeria, for instance, rebels have sabotaged oil pipelines and held oil platform workers hostage. In Colombia, a pipeline managed by Western oil companies is blown up on a regular basis. Nevertheless, some companies continue operating despite the violence. They can do this if the conflict is geographically isolated and contained or if it is not too severe. They may also decide that the government's policies toward the private sector are so favorable overall that the benefits outweigh the costs of conflict. If the industry is unlikely to be targeted by rebels or criminals, or can be structured financially in a way that reduces bottom-line risk, then the calculations may favor investment even in conflict-ridden territories (Berman 2000; Haufler 1997).[25]

In the extreme cases, for instance, the oil companies that continue operating in Burma despite the repressive military government there, activists pressure the companies to withdraw entirely (Earth Rights International 2000). But if a company makes the calculation to stay, its management may develop a corporate code to establish guidelines for its operations under those extreme conditions, similar to the guidelines established under the Sullivan Principles for apartheid South Africa. Certainly, outside pressure from activists will help push them in that direction. Shell executives faced this sort of calculation after the intense criticism they faced for their perceived complicity with the military government in Nigeria after the hanging of Ogoni activists there.

Extreme situations involving violence are not the only ones that force companies to consider adopting self-regulatory guidelines. Most business leaders also constantly assess the likelihood of government regulation as one of the major political risks they face. They view government regulation as a burden and a cost to be avoided if at all possible. There are, of course, situations in which an industry or set of firms prefers government intervention to restrain competition or promote consumer confidence. But this typically happens at the national level, where industry representatives may feel they have more control over the political process. They face more uncertainty about the transnational aspects of their corporate operations. The company may face the possibility of at least three sources of regulation: regulation in one or more host countries where the company operates; regulation by the home country of activities both at home *and* abroad; and international regulation.

How high is that risk currently? In recent years, most governments have sought to liberalize, deregulate, and privatize national economies. As one legal expert noted, "Almost all of these reforms are market-oriented; that is, they either substitute markets and the private sector for regulatory regimes or have public agencies use market approaches, structures and incentives to achieve their regulatory goals" (Aman 1999, 267). The re-regulation that has occurred is oriented toward making the state more competitive and often involves public-private partnerships or co-regulation. The EU, for instance, now delegates much regional standard setting to the private sector, and the U.S. government also has reduced or eliminated government action in some areas in favor of the market (Egan 1998; Harrison 1999).[26] At the national level, the political risk of regulation generally has declined, but recent changes tend to favor and encourage self-regulation by business interests. In many cases corporate voluntary initiatives are designed to reaffirm that indeed the government does not need to intervene; it is a defensive mechanism to prevent regulation. This attitude is most clear in new information technology sectors, which are not highly regulated, and industry players plan to keep it that way if they can.

One would expect most transnational companies to favor global rules, so that they would not have to deal with such a welter of conflicting national regulatory systems.[27] But the process of negotiating intergovernmental agreements can be slow, clumsy, often wrongheaded, and highly political, which means the design of rules—even rules that the private sector desires—can be fraught with risk. Some corporate decision makers may prefer instead to calculate how to use the differences in national regulation to gain a competitive advantage. For instance, different companies can take advantage of variations in the way that national regulatory systems affect the skills and wages of the labor pool.

In recent years, governments have been relatively successful at concluding new international agreements. Some of the most significant require action by the private sector. The Montreal Protocol on Substances that Deplete the Ozone Layer, negotiated in 1987, requires corporations to eliminate the production or emissions of ozone-depleting gases. The new Chemical Weapons Convention, negotiated in 1992, places strict new reporting requirements on the chemical industry.[28] At the regional level, the EU is harmonizing a host of regulations that affect its member countries, which also puts limits on European firms. In North America, the United States insisted on incorporating environmental and labor side agreements into the NAFTA treaty and recently has concluded a free trade agreement with Jordan that has similar conditions. Member governments of the OECD recently revised the Guidelines on Multinational Enterprises, successfully agreeing on a comprehensive international framework.[29] These all indicate a renewed risk of international regulation. Given this trend, some business leaders will consider implementing self-regulation in an effort to slow down or stop these intergovernmental efforts.

The final and newest factor in the political risk equation is the risk of transnational activist pressure. Until recently, most companies discounted the effect of social mobilization on their operations. They calculated that they could win their position through lobbying national governments, litigating in the courts, or stonewalling. Recent successes by activist groups in raising the costs of doing business through boycotts, shareholder activism, media campaigns, and litigation have changed this calculation (Broad and Cavanagh 1998). Shell lost a substantial amount of business when it tried to dispose of an old oil platform in the North Sea and Greenpeace launched an extensive and successful European campaign against it, using both media exposure and boycotts. In the United States, activists are using the Alien Tort Claims Act to bring companies to court over human rights violations abroad, effectively using litigation as a tool against the companies (Amon 2000; Morrin 2000).

Shareholder activism is on the rise as well. Socially responsible investment (SRI) funds, which screen out corporations deemed illegitimate in some way, are growing ever larger. Some major institutional investors, such as the California Pension System (Calpers), are now considering social screens too.[30] This kind of shareholder activism is primarily found in the United States, United Kingdom, Canada, and Australia.[31] In the United States, over $2 trillion is now handled by SRI funds, and over 120 institutions and mutual fund families have used their ownership of assets to bring shareholder resolutions on social issues (Social Investment Forum 2000). The U.S.-based Interfaith Center on Corporate Responsibility (ICCR) coordinates the shareholder votes of 275 religious institutional investors and has submitted hundreds of shareholder resolutions at company annual meetings (Oxford Analytica 2000). SRI had been small scale in Great Britain, but a recent survey of the top 500 British occupational pension funds showed that 59 percent of them, representing 78 percent of assets, had some form of SRI policy (Moon and Thamotheram 2000). Another survey in

2000 found that 71 percent of the financial community in London believes social and ethical considerations are more of a consideration for them today than five years ago, and 77 percent expect them to become more so in the coming five years (Opinion Leader Research 2000, 6).

The trigger for all these different forms of social mobilization might be the actions of a repressive government in a country where a foreign company operates, as in the case of Shell in Nigeria. Or, it might be some high profile action by the company itself, such as the Union Carbide chemical disaster in Bhopal, India. In turn, this mobilization can lead to a higher risk of government regulation. In many cases, corporate executives have great difficulty evaluating the potential impact of activism against them and what the costs might be. Many of them get it wrong. Shell had no idea that anyone would care if it dumped a retired oil platform in the deep sea and was blindsided by the Greenpeace campaign. As one recent corporate consulting report put it, there is "no hiding place" today for any business (Bray 1999). One response to these risks is to engage in more dialogue with activist groups and to try to meet their concerns through codes and guidelines that set standards for corporate behavior.

Joining these political risks, and interacting with them, are a number of significant economic risks that can also drive a company to adopt higher standards. One of the most obvious is the competitive position of the company or industry on a global basis. When markets are highly competitive, every added cost is harder for management to justify in terms of bottom-line profits and market share. Self-regulatory programs often entail significant financial costs and may undermine a firm's competitive position—especially if no other major market player adopts similar standards. This is the reason why it is difficult for a single corporation to adopt a highly restrictive code of conduct. When corporations can agree on setting standards together, however, the competitive position of each is maintained. Consequently, oligopolistic markets might be the most likely candidates for collective self-regulatory action, because it is easier to get a smaller number of firms to agree (Olson 1965). At the same time, the costs of self-regulation can be offset by significant benefits in terms of new markets for high-quality goods and services, or lower costs of production. For instance, if a company sets a higher standard for the elimination of industrial waste it may discover greater efficiencies in the production process.

Another economic risk that influences the decision to self-regulate is the degree to which the business of a company is tied to a specific locale, people, or production process (what economists call "asset-specificity").[32] Assets tied in this way are difficult if not impossible to disentangle. For instance, extractive industries such as mining are literally tied to the places where the minerals exist. They cannot really engage in a competitive race to the bottom, since they cannot move. The investments that mineral companies make are very large and usually long term. They are unlikely to leave a particular location voluntarily, even when the political situation around them deteriorates. This puts them in a unique political and economic position, subjecting them to more attention from activists and more regulation from governments. A company that cannot pick up and move must learn to manage the risk of transnational activism and government regulation. Other industry sectors, such as consumer goods manufacturing, have very low asset specificity. These firms often collaborate closely with a chain of suppliers around the world and yet maintain their distance and ability to drop one supplier and pick up another fairly easily. They can reduce the risk of too much specialization or dependence through outsourcing and business partnerships. These more flexible organizations should be less subject to political pressure of all kinds; for this very reason, long supply chains are themselves the object of intense criticism.[33]

Neither competitive pressures nor the threat of government regulation and public activism, however, can entirely explain the convergence across sectors and issues on a self-regulatory strategy. For one thing, in many cases the threat of government regulation has been relatively low. For another, transnational activism can be erratic, and the costs of dealing with it can be difficult to evaluate or relatively small compared to the scale of transnational business operations. Competitive pressures in most markets have increased, not decreased, in the past few decades. Yet we see corporations adopting codes and other practices in some of the most highly competitive markets today, including the information technology sector. Asset-specific production as a proportion of total production has declined as many economies shift to a postindustrial, information-based structure, and many consumer-oriented companies are part of a large and constantly evolving network of producers. The wave of mergers and acquisitions in the 1990s may mean that markets are highly concentrated, dominated by a few mega-corporations. But corporate codes are common even in markets with many competing firms and little concentration of economic activity. Two further factors are key elements of the self-regulatory trend: reputation and learning.

Reputation as a Global Corporate Asset

When a company develops a reputation for making a quality product, this gives the company a stronger brand name. Increasingly, we see competition in many markets based not just on how cheap a product is but also on the quality of the product. Corporations that are close to the consumer and sell directly to them are likely to feel bottom-line effects when consumers shun them if they believe the firm has behaved reprehensibly. There may even be emerging in some markets a "race to the top" among firms in global markets, instead of a race to the bottom, as each firm tries to become a market leader based on its reputation (Spar 1998). Reputation affects not just sales to customers, but also a range of other relationships on the production side as well. A company with a positive reputation is also attractive to potential employees; in tight labor markets, it can be an advantage in hiring those who favor working for firms with a strong positive image.

A company with a good reputation may also be able to make deals with other businesses more easily, because potential partners will want to be associated with the reputable firm or may simply trust it more.[34] Reputation matters in business-to-business relations, especially for industries that are organized in networks, in which trust facilitates contractual relations (Gomes-Casseres 1994). Particular sectors depend on reputation for their very existence. For instance, the financial sector depends on public confidence in the banking system, and it has been at the forefront in developing self-regulatory initiatives through industry associations (Cutler, Haufler, and Porter 1999).

In addition to consumers, employees, and business partners, a company's reputation also influences its relationship with government. In general, a good reputation makes it more likely that policy makers will try to avoid regulating an industry, or will regulate it in ways that are market friendly. The bad reputation of the tobacco industry has made it increasingly vulnerable to extensive government regulation—both national and international. A reputation as a good corporate citizen can lighten the regulatory burden on a company, make it more likely that government will be willing to delegate authority to the industry, or make them more accepting of industry self-regulation as an alternative to traditional command-and-control regulation. One reason that the U.S. government has been so favorable to self-regulation by information industries is that these industries have gained a reputation for innovation and economic dynamism, but they are still too new to have any old "baggage" from bad behavior in the past. In countries that have an institutional culture that tries to separate the business and political worlds, such as in the United States and United Kingdom, this kind of reputation may be more important than in countries with long histories of close cooperation between business and government on regulatory matters, such as continental Europe.

Once reputation becomes a significant asset of a company, that company will be more vulnerable to activist campaigns. Many NGO critics use the leverage of corporate reputation to try to influence the company's behavior. In response, a company may try to enhance its reputation even further by setting high standards in a variety of areas. This can be a two-edged sword: a firm that tries to develop a reputation for social responsibility often attracts attention—both to its successes *and* to its failures. However, it is often through developing a good reputation that a company can seek out NGOs for partnership and dialogue. In any case, the more a company values its reputation, the more likely it will be to try to preserve it and promote it through a variety of corporate codes and other voluntary initiatives.

Information, Knowledge, and Learning

The trend toward industry self-regulation would not be pushed forward very far without the spread of knowledge, information, and ideas within the business community regarding the relative costs and benefits of voluntary initiatives. Any self-regulatory system requires some consensus on what the rules ought to be and expertise on how to implement them (Gordon 1999, 9). In the case of self-regulation, corporate leaders are developing common knowledge that they use to change their policy projects and political strategies.[35] Industry self-regulation is still at a relatively early stage of development, so there are only scattered areas of consensus that vary across issue areas. In those areas where there is some agreement over appropriate norms and standards, managers are more likely to self-regulate. Where consensus is deep, self-regulation is likely to be negotiated and implemented collectively.

The role of leadership in this process should not be underestimated. Leading executives may adopt new strategies, lobby other business leaders to join them, and even put economic pressure on business partners through their business relationships, such as supply networks. These leaders can be especially effective if they dominate their markets. For instance, when it comes to the issue of climate change, John Browne of BP Amoco has taken a prominent stand in favor of early action to stop global warming. Others take a broader view, instead of focusing on one specific issue they argue in favor of taking a "triple-bottom-line" approach to business, in which the bottom line is measured in terms of the company's profits, effect on social values, and impact on the environment (Elkington 1998). These new ideas and approaches can be reinforced by business education programs. Certain business schools now teach required courses in business ethics and social responsibility. In addition, trade magazines address issues of best practice as an aspect of quality management within a firm, and many consultants and authors regularly publish articles or give lectures on how a firm can gain value by setting high standards.

In the past few decades, businesses have created organizations dedicated to spreading information and knowledge about these ideas while highlighting their leadership on these issues. The World Business Council for Sustainable Development (WBCSD), composed of leading MNCs, requires its members to commit voluntarily to promote sustainable development, which the WBCSD defines quite broadly. There are no sanctions for those members who violate this commitment and there is little monitoring. But the WBCSD provides training, guidance, technical assistance, and information on sustainable practices to its members and highlights the importance of adhering to good business practices. Business leaders and industry associations establish business "best practices," and these influence what other managers view as the normal range of options available to them.

THE VOLUNTARY ADOPTION of social standards by an increasing number of companies presents a different picture of the role of the corporation in world affairs. Observers and participants alike point out that the standards these companies establish are often higher than national or international ones. They address contentious public policy issues and not just technical standards that only concern industry. When companies establish their own rules and standards in sociopolitical areas, these can complement or supplement government regulation, especially in countries with weak capacity to regulate. International standard setting fills in the gaps where national regulatory systems conflict or remain silent. Where governments do not govern, the private sector does—often in response to the demands of public interest groups who find themselves unable to move national governments. And when governments are unwilling or unable to govern effectively, political leaders may see private governance as a valuable tool to achieve public ends.

National policy makers are beginning to pay attention to the possible benefits of industry self-regulation. They may hope that as business improves its behavior abroad then government will be under less pressure to act against the private sector at home or abroad. They may also hope to use corporate social responsibility as a tool to promote "soft" foreign policy goals, such as human development. The United States, United Kingdom, and Canada have promoted better international business practices in the past decade. Canada has developed an International Code of Ethics for Canadian Business, the United States has its Model Business Principles, and the United Kingdom has launched an Ethical Trading Initiative—all aimed to set high standards for corporate behavior overseas. Probably the most significant initiative in this regard is the Global Compact between the United Nations and multinational business. UN Secretary-General Kofi Annan in 1999 challenged business to adopt the principles enunciated in UN conventions regarding labor rights, human rights, and environmental protection.[36]

Industry self-regulation of corporate activities abroad is driven by a number of cross-cutting factors. These factors include the risk of being targeted for regulation or for attention from transnational activists. They also include the growing importance of corporate reputation in relations with consumers, business partners, employees, and policy makers. Policy makers and the public at large might support and promote these efforts simply because of the lack of capacity of many foreign governments to govern effectively or democratically, and the fact that traditional foreign policy tools such as sanctions rarely change any government's policies. The increasing visibility of differences in living conditions across countries as modern media enter the homes of millions has led to a backlash against globalization and a compelling need to do something to mitigate its effects. In this context, many different groups see the potential for leveraging the corporation by manipulating corporate risks, reputation, and learning.

Governments that want to promote industry self-regulation can do so by leveraging their power to threaten to regulate. They can also facilitate transnational activism by ensuring that information about corporate actions is available to the public. Policy makers also can heighten the effectiveness of reputation as a tool of regulation by supporting the monitoring, accounting, and certification programs that help measure and reinforce reputation. A key element of industry self-regulation is that business leaders must be educated about the value of raising their own standards, about the costs of refusing to act on those standards, and about the appropriate standards and implementation measures they should undertake.

There cannot, however, be a one-size-fits-all approach. Industry self-regulation is in general a positive development, but it cannot resolve all the thorny international political issues. In many cases, the problem is the weakness of governance at the international and national levels. Private sector governance, then, is only a second-best solution. There is broad public consensus on overarching norms and principles for international business behavior, but little agreement on how to implement them on the ground.

2

The Case of International Environmental Protection

IN THE UNITED STATES and other industrialized countries, environmental issues are some of the most contentious problems policy makers face. From water pollution to ozone depletion to global warming, society faces an array of daunting choices about how to reconcile a modern industrial economy with the evident harm to the natural environment. In the past three decades, the United States and many countries in Europe erected an extensive regulatory system to clean up the air, water, and land. Some newly industrializing countries are only beginning to develop an environmental regulatory system, while many others ignore environmental concerns in their efforts to achieve high economic growth rates.

For transnational environmental problems, the alternatives of international regulation, domestic regulation, and industry self-regulation can be held up in sharp contrast. Taking a broad view, it appears that all three approaches have been tested to their greatest extent for environmental issues. In the past decade, numerous international environmental agreements have been negotiated. Domestic environmental regulation has widespread support in public opinion polls, and most industrialized countries and an increasing number of developing ones regulate industry's impact on the environment.[37] At the same time, a significant number of companies are signing up for a variety of self-regulatory programs developed internally or pushed by industry associations and outside groups.

This chapter examines the factors pushing companies to adopt self-regulatory practices that address international environmental issues. The first section describes environmental self-regulation, focusing on initiatives that span national borders. The next section examines more closely the political and economic risks that dominate the debates over environmental codes and practices by business. This discussion also addresses the ways in which political and economic risks interact with the increasing importance of reputation in business affairs, and how all of these contribute to the learning process that is going on within the business community. The final section analyzes the issues of enforcement, accountability, and participation in environmental self-regulation.

Environmental Codes, Management Systems, and Programs

Environmental protection is an issue area made up of an array of overlapping subissues. This means that the debates between companies and their critics are often broken up into narrower slices of argument, and there is no clear set of principles around which consensus can emerge. When we speak about action on environmental issues, we are usually talking about reducing or eliminating emissions of wastes, such as greenhouse gases, oil spills, or toxic chemicals; and decreasing or eliminating the profligate exploitation of natural materials in production, such as logging and mining. Related to these material considerations are the more human ones: concerns about how environmental degradation affects income, ethnic conflict, indigenous-group rights, and human rights in general. All of these issues constitute the arena of environmental politics, and MNCs are right in the center of it.

Although a number of corporations may have made some reference to the environment in their policy statements decades ago, we can date the real beginning of international self-regulatory initiatives to the response to two major disasters: the Union Carbide chemical disaster in Bhopal, India, in 1984, and the *Exxon Valdez* oil spill in 1989.[38] Both of these disasters provided fuel for the corporate accountability movement, and activists became energized by the scale and scope of these horrific disasters. Each of these led to the construction of different kinds of codes of conduct.

The city of Bhopal is now widely known as the site of one of the worst chemical disasters in history. In 1984, a Union Carbide India plant released 40 tons of lethal chemicals into the surrounding community. Thousands of people died or were severely injured.[39] Union Carbide was mercilessly attacked in the press, paid millions of dollars in damages to the Indian government, and was the object of extensive litigation. The rest of the chemical industry was horrified, both by the accident itself and by its political aftermath. The Canadian Chemical Association developed a collective response, setting forth the "Responsible Care" set of standards for handling toxic chemicals. Responsible Care then was internationalized, with the International Council of Chemical Associations (ICCA) overseeing the program. It has been adopted now by over 40 national chemical associations from around the world. This program requires a company to ensure that it has a commitment to environmental, health, and safety values; implements those values through codes, guidelines, and checklists; establishes indicators to measure progress; communicates effectively with employees and the community; adopts a Responsible Care logo and identity; and persuades others to join. In 1996, the ICCA added a final, significant feature: verification of progress. The program clearly aims to standardize practices around the world to ensure that no more Bhopals ever occur. Members who violate the provisions of Responsible Care can be kicked out of the industry association. This penalty is rarely invoked, because the members prefer to work with offenders to persuade them to raise their standards and train them to do so. Some individual members have gone on to develop internal self-evaluation programs to monitor their own implementation processes, and many admit that a better-enforced system must eventually be adopted. Industry associations are reluctant to punish noncomplying members or make public their violations. Critics argue that Responsible Care is designed to promote the environmental image of the industry, fight off government regulation, and promote Responsible Care itself.

Whereas the Bhopal disaster led to a collective response by the chemical industry, the *Exxon Valdez* oil spill led to a collective response by public interest advocates. The 1989 accident dumped 10.8 million gallons into Prince William Sound in Alaska. It is the largest spill in U.S. history, and some argue it is the largest worldwide in terms of its damage to the environment.[40] The environmental community mobilized to retaliate against Exxon, boycotted its products, pursued litigation, and lobbied for government regulation. A group of investors, pension funds, foundations, labor unions, and environmental, religious, and public interest groups immediately drew up a set of principles in 1989 for industry to adopt. These were originally called the Valdez Principles but are now known as the CERES Principles.[41] They lay out guidelines for corporate environmental responsibility, including the protection of the biosphere, sustainable enterprise, conservation, and—significantly—a commitment to auditing and reporting.[42] CERES works with corporations to try to persuade them to adopt the Principles. To date, over 50 corporations are members of CERES, including twelve major MNCs, among them General Motors, Polaroid, Bethlehem Steel, Sun Oil, and others.

The Responsible Care program and the CERES Principles are both collective responses (albeit by different actors). In addition, many corporations responded individually by developing their own codes of conduct. These company-specific codes became increasingly common throughout the 1990s. Shell, for instance, developed an extensive in-house process to revise and publicize its code of conduct after its public image was blackened first by its passivity in the face of repression in Nigeria and then by its plans to dispose of an oil platform in the North Sea. Corporate employees at all levels contributed to developing the new code, and Shell proudly published its final principles. The Shell code pays particular attention to environmental responsibility. Today, Shell is also willing to make public an annual report of its environmental performance. Its latest report, entitled "How Do We Stand? People, Planet, and Profits," provides data on economic, environmental, and social performance. The Shell report indicates that company facilities have reduced greenhouse gas emissions, participated in conservation projects, are developing cleaner fuels, and are slowly shifting from coal to natural gas as a primary fuel source (Royal Dutch/ Shell 2000). It also reflects the areas in which the corporation has failed to improve. Shell also participates in a wide range of organizations that promote corporate social responsibility.

Throughout the 1980s, many companies began developing a more technical or organizational approach to dealing with environmental problems. To implement their corporate codes, they developed environmental management systems (EMS). An EMS is designed to strengthen the internal organizational accountability of a corporation by linking the company's environmental policy statement to actual lines of command to ensure that the policy is implemented. As more and more companies adopted a variety of EMS, critics argued that the lack of common standards meant that many EMS programs had little meaning or effect, especially in developing countries. The British government decided it should set voluntary EMS standards to complement its regulatory regime. At about the same time, the EU developed its own Eco-Management and Audit Scheme (EMAS). These EMS appeared attractive to both governments and industry, because they were technical, voluntary, and process-oriented.

By 1990, an array of environmentally oriented voluntary initiatives existed, although they were often incompatible, weakly enforced, and vague. The business community had become more aware of the transnational mobilization of NGOs and more sensitive to their environmental demands. This was crystallized by the UN Conference on Environment and Development (UNCED), set to begin in Rio de Janeiro, Brazil, in 1992. Many NGOs had a direct hand in the preparations for the conference, but the business community initially did not understand the importance this conference would attain. During the early stages, however, Maurice Strong, Secretary-General of the conference and a former businessman, realized that the business community needed to mobilize to address the far-reaching nature of these negotiations, and he encouraged the formation of an organization to represent multinational corporate interests.

The newly formed Business Council for Sustainable Development (later to become the World Business Council for Sustainable Development, or WBCSD) sent representatives to Rio to promote a business agenda on sustainable development. Business interests had finally awakened to the effective way in which NGOs were setting the international environmental agenda. At the Rio conference, business interests advocated EMS as a voluntary self-regulatory mechanism that governments should support. Many activists opposed the participation of business groups at Rio and argued that they weakened and undermined the proposals being negotiated. An important outcome of Rio, largely due to business lobbying, was the explicit recognition of the potential role of voluntary industry initiatives in addressing sustainable development issues. Agenda 21, the centerpiece of the conference, provided a broad plan of action and contained language encouraging business and others to strengthen voluntary initiatives through free market mechanisms and incentives. It recommends that industry should pursue new avenues of cleaner production and promote "responsible entrepreneurship" (UNCED 1992). Following UNCED, the WBCSD developed a set of voluntary guidelines for its members. WBCSD members commit to uphold the best environmental practices, sustainable enterprise, and especially self-regulation. Member companies sign on to these principles, but there is no strong enforcement mechanism. The WBCSD works hard to educate and persuade companies of the benefits of eco-efficiency, producing reports, case studies, and training programs. The members of the WBCSD are MNCs, and they are all encouraged to go beyond compliance with national law to achieve higher standards. The WBCSD has become a well-established promoter of sustainable industry in a variety of world forums.

In the past decade, business leaders have created a number of other organizations similar to the WBCSD. These include the Prince of Wales Business Leaders Forum (PWBLF) based in London; Business for Social Responsibility (BSR) in San Francisco; and the Pew Center for Climate Change in Washington, D.C. Each promotes corporate social responsibility and voluntary initiatives, laying out broad expectations and providing information and model cases for members to use in developing their own corporate codes. BSR and PWBLF principles address a broad range of issues beyond environmental ones, and the Pew Center focuses specifically on climate change.

To follow up on Agenda 21, many business leaders recognized the need to establish more international consensus on what exactly an EMS should look like. For a variety of political reasons, the negotiations over this landed in the hands of the ISO, the central body for negotiating and promoting technical industry standards.[43] In 1991, the ISO had begun to consider developing an EMS standard—not realizing at first the degree of difference between technical and socio-environmental standard setting. The ISO is an international organization whose members are national standard-setting bodies, which may be private or public sector agencies. The actual design of standards is in the hands of technical committees, typically dominated by industry representatives, with one national body acting as host to the negotiations. The standards are adopted voluntarily by corporations but often become a de facto requirement for doing business.

Over the course of the 1990s, the ISO negotiated what it called the ISO 14000 EMS standards, first published in 1996. The ISO 14000 establishes guidelines for a process for ensuring that a corporate environmental policy is implemented, but they do not set limits on pollutant output.[44] Signatories are reviewed on a plant-by-plant basis by outside auditors for ISO certification. At first, many businesses were slow to adopt the new standards. Some countries worried about the cost to their industries. U.S. companies believed that U.S. law held them to even higher standards than those set out by the ISO 14000. Because many environmental groups did not support ISO 14000, they did not pressure companies to adopt it. This quickly changed, however. Many European companies are now certified, with East Asian companies following closely behind. Japanese companies have the highest number of environmental certifications, while North and South America lag behind (Chemical Market Reporter 1999; Hogarth 1999). The rate at which certifications are awarded nearly doubled in 1999. ISO 14000 certifications have also been awarded in such unexpected places as Afghanistan (ISO 2000). Rapidly industrializing countries in East Asia believe that certification will demonstrate to buyers abroad that they can meet world standards and compete in world markets. Between 1996 and 1997, the number of certifications jumped by close to 40 percent, covering facilities in 129 countries. The electrical equipment industry leads in ISO 14000 certifications (ISO 2000). Recently, both General Motors and Ford Motor Company declared that all their suppliers would have to be certified to the ISO 14000 standards. Today, ISO 14000 is fast becoming a requirement for doing business in world markets (Haufler 1999).[45]

During the 1990s, there has almost been a kind of "contagion effect" within industries, as more and more adopt codes of conduct and EMS. This did not just occur in the United States, but also in other areas of the world. In Canada, the oil and extractive industries in particular began developing their own self-regulatory commitments (English 2000, 4).[46] Almost every company that has a corporate code or mission statement now includes some reference to environmental standards. More and more industry associations have developed "green" programs of various sorts. For example, the International Hotels Environmental Initiative was established in 1993 by twelve leading hotel chains. Hotels are huge consumers of everything from carpet and towels to food and landscaping. The initiative supplies hoteliers with guidelines on how to operate in an environmentally sustainable manner. The World Travel and Tourism Council organized Green Globe, which hands out awards for environmental excellence and is developing a certification system called the Green Globe Standard, based on Agenda 21. More hotels and travel operators will adopt these programs if MNCs require their travel departments to seek out hotels that meet environmental standards, and large hotel chains become more savvy buyers of sustainable products and processes. To date, these initiatives have had mixed effects in terms of actual outcomes. Even when a company adopts the standards, its subsidiaries or local management may be given a free hand on whether or not to implement them.

One of the most significant trends in industry self-regulation is what might be considered "programmatic" initiatives created in partnership with NGOs and international organizations. These include the Forest Stewardship Council (FSC), the Marine Stewardship Council, the Climate Initiative of the World Resources Institute, and the World Commission on Dams. All of these involve direct partnership between industry and public interest groups. The FSC, for instance, is a nonprofit organization founded in 1993 through negotiations among multiple stakeholders, including the timber industry. It promotes sustainable use of forests around the world by evaluating and accrediting certifiers, by developing forest management standards, and by educating business and the public on the issue of deforestation (FSC US 2000). Home Depot is now one of the largest supporters of the program, having bowed to activists demanding that it stop selling uncertified wood products. Other major wood products stores have followed suit, starting a ripple effect on retailers and their worldwide suppliers. "There is no question that the FSC has absolutely changed the fabric of the industry," claims a forest-products consultant (Carlton 2000).[47] The number of acres certified went from 2 to 45 million in the course of five years. The Marine Stewardship Council is similar, and in recent years, a number of large buyers and processors of fish have signed on to it (Marine Stewardship Council 2000).

Throughout the 1990s, more and more activists pressed corporations to issue public reports on the effects of their operations on the environment. Over the course of the decade, numerous companies began to do so, but the standards for these reports varied dramatically.

Today, about 50 percent of U.S. Fortune 500 companies produce environmental reports, and the quality of those reports is steadily improving (Investor Responsibility Research Center 2000). In many cases, the financial sector is demanding better environmental reporting by corporations, especially the SRI funds (Adams 1998).

In the mid-1990s, CERES brought together representatives from industry, accounting and auditing firms, and public interest groups under the umbrella of the UNEP to develop common reporting standards. This effort, known as the Global Reporting Initiative (GRI), has made significant progress in developing a common set of indicators and a format for public reporting. Although public environmental reports are not yet commonplace, there does appear to be a significant trend favoring their use. Once a company commits to environmental reporting, it takes a step forward that is difficult to reverse. Just to make such a report, a company has to assess how its operations affect the natural environment, something about which most companies know little. BP Amoco, for instance, made a commitment to reduce its emission of greenhouse gases. Once it did so, it first had to figure out how to measure such emissions and then actually measure them at all of its worldwide facilities. When that was done, a public report could be made—and outsiders could evaluate how well BP Amoco was meeting its commitments. In its 1999 public report, BP Amoco's figures showed that the company reduced emissions in some facilities, but due to the growth in production, the final result did not reach the company's target (BP Amoco 2000). Once the initial investment in measurement, evaluation, and reporting is made, the company will try to make sure that there is progress from one report to the next.

The issue of climate change has generated some of the most interesting industry activities. UNCED galvanized corporations into adopting corporate codes and EMS. But it also laid out the path for future negotiations over reducing emissions of greenhouse gases. Initially the Global Climate Coalition appeared to be the most visible industry presence at these negotiations, and its members adamantly opposed any action to enforce limits on carbon emissions. In response, Greenpeace and UNEP together helped organize a counter-coalition of financial and insurance industries, which could face enormous losses from changes in climate and weather (Leggett 1996). Industry representatives signed on to the UNEP Statement by Financial Institutions on the

Environment and Sustainable Development. It has over 115 signatories, and a similar one exists for the insurance industry. As part of their commitments, many of the companies are now implementing programs to reduce their carbon emissions. A few insurance companies are also contemplating decreasing prices on insurance coverage for customers who follow sustainable business practices.

By the turn of the century, the field of environmental regulation included an expanding array of private sector self-regulatory initiatives. Almost every major MNC—and many small- and medium-sized corporations too—now has in place some form of corporate code of environmental conduct. Over time, an increasing number have also implemented EMS to facilitate the implementation of environmental policy. Thousands of facilities around the world are now certified to ISO 14000 standards. Major, highly visible corporations such as Shell and BP Amoco have made sustainability their watchword. Prominent MNCs now participate in a wide variety of business groups supporting environmental principles, from signing on to the CERES Principles to supporting the UNEP Statement.

Risk, Reputation, and Learning

Environmental issues demonstrate clearly how risk, reputation, and learning interact in the evolving world of industry self-regulation. Two political risks are particularly salient in the environmental arena: the threat of government regulation and the effectiveness of transnational activism. OECD countries generally have effective national environmental regulatory systems. In some countries in Europe, Green parties have won support at the polls for maintaining and even expanding those systems. The real problem for industry comes from abroad: managers must decide whether or not to apply equally high standards in other countries where they operate, or whether to engage in "regulatory arbitrage," that is, to seek out the location with the most compatible set of regulations.

The international context is, however, deeply intertwined with national trends. In the environmental policy arena, many national governments are experimenting with both carrots and sticks: carrots in the form of incentives for industry self-regulation; sticks in the form of traditional regulatory rules. The United States, United Kingdom, and especially New Zealand have been at the forefront of this trend. Policy makers are trying to develop a way to enhance national economic competitiveness while meeting popular demands for environmental protection. New Zealand has probably gone the farthest in privatizing its environmental regulatory system, but co-regulation and delegation to the private sector have become common in many countries (Egan 1998). New policies often include explicit promotion of industry self-regulation, with the threat of traditional command-and-control measures backing them up (Harrison 1999).

Internationally, we can see a similar carrot-and-stick pattern: international negotiators at Kyoto proposed both strict limits on carbon emissions and more market-friendly devices such as carbon emissions permit trading. These national and international developments encourage industry to adopt voluntary initiatives, both to take advantage of the incentives and to try to prevent the imposition of government rules. This dynamic between the state and the private sector in OECD countries does not necessarily apply in developing countries, however. Often, even if there are good rules on the books, a developing country government does not have the will or capacity to enforce them. As one observer recently stated, "We Latin Americans . . . like laws and regulations. We put a lot of effort into them, but we never carry them out" (DeYoung and Nelson 2000, 18).[48] This means that the combination of incentives and threats is not as powerful in developing countries as elsewhere. The stick in non-OECD countries often is local and international activist pressure. Porter and Brown, two well-known experts on the environment, point out that corporations have their greatest political influence when there are no negotiations going on over a formal, binding international regime governing an environmental issue. In those circumstances, business typically does not see a need for self-regulation and in fact may use their clout with national governments and international organizations to protect their freedom of maneuver (Porter and Brown 1996, 63).

Transnational activist networks have become increasingly visible, especially in lobbying for international action on environmental concerns (Wapner 1996; Keck and Sikkink 1998). They have become more skilled at mobilizing their members and shaping public opinion.

Many of the environmental activists in Europe and the United States are reaching out to their counterparts in the developing world, cultivating ties with them. They have been particularly effective in creating coalitions with indigenous groups who are often the most vulnerable to foreign investors invading their lands for oil or minerals (Burke 1999). These activists have framed the policy debates successfully in terms of a perceived race to the bottom and "environmental dumping" in developing countries. Hundreds if not thousands of environmental activist organizations coordinate their political campaigns to address environmental problems in a globally concerted manner.[49]

The Rio Conference marked a turning point in putting environmental issues on the global agenda, and it mobilized a tremendous number of NGOs. In the 1990s, states successfully negotiated a number of far-reaching environmental agreements, including the ambitious Montreal Protocol on Substances that Deplete the Ozone Layer in 1992 and, less successfully, the Kyoto Protocol on climate change in 1998. The EU has been extremely active in harmonizing regulations across its member states. The United States has insisted on incorporating environmental side agreements into recent regional and bilateral trade treaties, such as NAFTA and Jordan. The Group of Eight Industrialized Countries (G-8) ministers recently agreed to link trade and environment issues in the next round of trade talks. All of these add up to a rising probability of international regulation, which business interests may take as a warning that they need to raise their own environmental standards if they want to prevent or slow down international regulatory trends. The intertwining of regulatory and activist risk has helped push the private sector to consider seriously the benefits of adopting voluntary standards.

One of the striking features of environmental issues is that economic risk is, in many cases, less of a problem for the private sector here than it is in other issue areas. Functioning environmental markets have emerged in the last decade that can make industry efforts to adopt sustainable practices profitable. They were constructed in part as a result of international and national regulatory changes, such as the creation of markets in pollution permits (Haas 1999). Both government regulation and popular concern for green products and processes made it easier for companies to see a competitive advantage in pursuing higher standards in environmental protection. They are most advanced in the United States, Germany, and Japan but are growing elsewhere (Moore and Miller 1994; Haas 1999). These markets for products and technology that are green are only one aspect of environmental profitability. The other is changes in production processes that increase efficiency by reducing waste and pollution (Hawken et al. 2000).

Because environmental problems touch on such a wide range of producers, each segment of the market has different economic dynamics. Voluntary initiatives that commit a company, for instance, to reduce greenhouse gas emissions will face very different competitive dynamics than similar programs to reduce logging in rainforests. In each case, industry players have to make different calculations of the trade-offs between competitive and political pressures, both of which can affect market share and revenue streams. Oil and mining firms tend to be large, with relatively few competitors, but with intense competition among them. The petroleum sector in particular has responded to economic competition with a series of large mergers and acquisitions, as BP swallowed up Amoco and then Arco, and Exxon combined with Mobil. Within this relatively small group, BP Amoco views itself as an industry leader both in terms of size and more importantly in terms of business practices. John Browne, chief executive of BP Amoco, explicitly points to his corporation's environmental practices as a model for others to follow. He literally shocked the other oil companies by coming out in support of early action against global warming.

Other industries view demands that they become more green with varying degrees of concern about competitiveness. Most businesses today are more dependent on knowledge and communication, and less dependent on natural resources. Corporate executives of Shell, for instance, refer to the firm not only as a supplier of petroleum products but of transportation and information services also. Other more consumer-oriented companies are subject to a great deal of competition, and entry by competitors into particular markets can be easy. In highly competitive markets, firms are pushed in two directions, often simultaneously—to cut costs or to improve quality. Many have begun to enter green markets, becoming niche producers in a growing area of consumer interest. The companies that produce and sell environmentally friendly products must be able to show a demonstrable commitment to high environmental standards.

High visibility campaigns against poor environmental practices have been heightened by three intertwined factors: the growing importance of global brand name as an element of corporate competitiveness; the increasing transparency of corporate activities, whether deliberate or not; and the process of persuasion and learning among business interests themselves. It is clear that a good reputation only matters if it is possible that a bad reputation will affect relations with customers and business partners. Information about violations of acceptable environmental behavior must be widely available. Information transparency and reputation are linked. For instance, the Environmental Defense Fund (EDF) launched a campaign in 1998 to test common chemicals for health effects, asking major corporations to do the testing. The EDF published a list of those that said yes and those that said no. Shortly afterwards, in January 1999, the Chemical Manufacturers Association (CMA) in the United States announced it would spend $1 billion to gather toxicity and other data on 3,000 chemicals, and another 15,000 will be tested for their effects on the human endocrine system. The results will be posted on the CMA web site (Business Ethics 1999). In other words, simply the fact that the company name would be posted in the "negative" column of the EDF web site was enough to move the industry association to shore up its reputation and that of its members. A further step would be if these companies also committed to restrict their use of toxic chemicals. When the U.S. Environmental Protection Agency began requiring factories to report on their use of certain toxic substances and those data were publicized in the Toxics Release Inventory, many firms immediately began reducing their use of these chemicals.

Activist campaigns are not always directed to closed ears within the business community. Over the past few decades, there has been a learning process among certain managers that makes them more receptive to the idea of voluntary action to self-regulate at home and abroad (Prakash 2000). Many business schools now require students to take courses in business ethics and environmentalism. Scholars have persuasively demonstrated with empirical data that caring for the environment can be a profitable strategy. Leading businessmen and corporations have stepped forward to demonstrate the cutting edge in good company practice on the environment. Business leaders have created organizations to promote both individual and collective action on environmental issues. Many of these have an explicitly educational and persuasive mission to convince other businesses to join. CERES, the WBCSD, the Prince of Wales Business Leaders Forum, Business for Social Responsibility, the Global Environmental Management Initiative (GEMI), and others are nonprofit organizations made up of member companies who agree to promote a better understanding of environmental issues and to convince other firms to agree to meeting higher standards.

Probably the most persuasive aspect of the new corporate environmentalism is the "eco-efficiency paradigm." Many analysts point out that pollution as a by-product of industrial production is waste—pure and simple. Improving environmental performance can improve efficiency by reducing inputs into production and thus limiting waste by-products. In other words, environmental practices are not by definition a cost center for the firm, but they can also be a source of profit. Numerous examples now exist of practices that reduce consumption and pollution in ways that are financially sound. For instance, when semiconductor manufacturers sought a less toxic cleaner to use in the production process, they found that water-based products not only met higher environmental standards, but they worked better and more cheaply. Managers had simply been using old mental habits, automatically using traditional chemical cleaners without really thinking seriously about alternatives until pressured to do so (Hawken 1993). Environmentally sound products and production processes can provide an edge in highly competitive markets, as market leaders in resource-intensive industries are discovering. Green businesses have made environmental stewardship a core value of their business because, in many cases, it really works.[50]

Outside consultants, writers, and activists have been producing a proliferating number of persuasive guides about the benefits of pursuing sustainable industry. In the intriguingly titled *Cannibals with Forks*, John Elkington, a British management consultant, argues that firms should re-orient themselves to the "triple bottom line." Elkington, like many other authors and experts today, is trying to persuade business managers that they should be profitable in more than the financial dimension, taking into account social and environmental bottom lines (Elkington 1998). An increasing number of firms, especially in Europe, are adopting triple-bottom-line practices under The Natural Step program.[51] Business schools now incorporate environmental issues into the curriculum, and trade magazines—even the most conservative—now devote space to best environmental practice.[52] The dialogue in the business world today includes discussion, debate, and evolving acceptance of the role of good environmental practices in business decision making. This makes business leaders more receptive to public pressure to self-regulate.

Enforcement, Accountability, and Participation

Environmental self-regulation is making process in terms of the instruments of credibility and accountability already in place or being developed. Two elements of this are the degree to which corporations pursue internal and especially external verification of their environmental performance; and the degree to which companies now make the results of environmental audits public. For any firm or industry, verification measures and public reporting play to both the members of the organization and the wider public. Verification through EMS, accounting, and auditing allows management to make sure that internal organizational systems are performing correctly. It also permits benchmarking performance from one year to the next for a single firm and comparisons across competitors or across broader societal standards. For many firms, public reporting can be both a blessing and a curse. It allows a company that has adopted self-regulatory standards to develop a positive reputation. It can also provide the public with information to which they would not otherwise have access that can be used to assess whether the firm or industry has lived up to its commitments.

Initially, many environmental codes of conduct and other programs had little or no verification measures. Over the past decade, the business world has made significant progress in environmental accounting. These efforts cover such elements as emissions, energy usage, waste generation, and material use. Large companies may also report on environmental technology improvements, site remediation, research programs, employee incentives, and other organizational measures. These can be prepared internally, or by outside consultants, accountants, and auditors. The Responsible Care program initially relied only on self-assessment by member companies, but many member firms, particularly in the United States and Canada, are developing independent verification programs. In 1996, verification was added to the requirements of the program. The GEMI produced an Environmental Self-Assessment Program to assist companies in evaluating their performance against the International Chamber of Commerce (ICC) Business Charter principles. These results are not made public, but the process is one tool by which companies can assess their implementation of environmental programs. EMS, including ISO 14000, are another verification program. ISO 14000 requires that firms be audited and certified as compliant with the standards. The company must hire outside auditors for ISO certification. The exact results of an ISO 14000 assessment are not made public in most cases, although whether or not the company obtained certification is publicly available. External verification is an even stronger tool than internal EMS for improving corporate performance. In individual cases, a firm may work closely with a nonprofit group to evaluate its performance. Shell estimates its verification program cost over $2 million.

As part of triple-bottom-line corporate management, companies evaluate themselves against specific performance indicators, which include financial, environmental, and social indicators. Both Shell and The Body Shop are devising ways to report on triple-bottom-line performance. The WBCSD also has a program to consider how to add the social dimension to traditional financial reporting requirements by developing environmental and social "ledgers" with performance indicators, measurements, and evaluation guidelines. UNCTAD supports research into environmental accounting, which is a newly developing field of inquiry.

The next step after verification or measurement of performance is the decision of whether or not to make any of that information public. The Investor Responsibility Resource Center estimates that half the Fortune 500 companies now produce environmental reports. More than 2,000 organizations worldwide voluntarily publish environmental reports today (GRI 2000). Furthermore, the quality of the reports is improving, often through the efforts of collective groups. One example is the Public Environmental Reporting Initiative (PERI), launched in 1993 by nine North American companies, which lays out guidelines for public reporting. The 1997 UNEP/SustainAbility Benchmark Survey of 100 corporate environmental reports demonstrated dramatic progress in reporting. "Companies are now publishing data in ways which they actively argued would be commercially suicidal as recently as the early 1990s," says John Elkington, SustainAbility Chairman (UNEP and SustainAbility 1997). A group of nonprofit groups (such as CERES), accounting firms (such as Pricewaterhouse-Coopers), and business groups (such as ICC) have come together to negotiate a global framework for voluntary reporting of economic, environmental, and social performance. This Global Reporting Initiative is conducted under the auspices of UNEP with the goal of becoming a permanent new international organization in 2002. The participants —numbering over 1,000 from 35 countries—believe that a common framework will enhance the consistency, comparability, and credibility of reporting.[53] Unfortunately, consensus on the appropriate standards and requirements for effective reporting remains elusive, but at least more companies are willing to provide some information about the effects of their operations on the environment.[54]

Reporting is a key element to upgrading the effectiveness of self-regulation. It allows the public to make judgments about the degree to which companies are in fact meeting standards, improving their environmental performance, and ultimately reducing the damage they do to the natural world. Public reporting allows for feedback, dialogue, and—in the worst case—punishment. That punishment can be through public protest, actions such as boycotts and shareholder resolutions, or in some cases litigation. Companies that demonstrate progress can be rewarded, although to date the evidence indicates that the public is quick to punish and slow to reward. Much of the available environmental reporting is specific to a particular plant, product, or issue. Broader comparisons are still difficult to draw.

An analysis of corporate environmental programs indicates that they are becoming more institutionalized within many firms. Among a group of 261 companies, primarily market leaders, over half designate a vice president responsible for environmental affairs. About 92 percent have a formal corporate environmental policy in place, which in over half of the companies is backed up by monetary rewards in the form of compensation. Of the firms surveyed, 95 percent have environmental compliance auditing programs, reflecting that environmental issues are important for financial risk management (Adams 1998).

The effectiveness of efforts to promote environmental responsibility in the corporate world depends on the ability of specific firms to implement their commitments. With the best will in the world, many organizations simply face too many internal and external barriers to implementation. One recent study looked at how MNCs transfer the methods and tools of traditional business management to the newer areas of environmental, health, and safety management. Among other things, it noted that, organizationally, emphasis on environmental, health, and safety management was often an add-on and not well integrated with regular business systems (Yosie and Herbst 1998).

WHAT WOULD AN EFFECTIVE environmental self-regulatory system look like? One scholar argues it must include a commitment to sustainable development, as an integral part of corporate decision making and management; measurable goals for improving environmental performance; monitoring, assessment, and independent verification of performance; public reporting and mechanisms for transparency of environmental information; community consultation and partnership; a culture of environmental responsibility encouraged through management systems and staff training; compliance with legislation as the minimum, with a focus on continuous improvement and best practice; standards applied on a worldwide basis; and monitoring of implementation (Adams 1998).

No one would argue we are there yet. Not all would agree that the full panoply of elements listed here is really required. In any case, it is evident that, in general, the private sector has made some progress but has much farther to go before the public has full confidence in these voluntary initiatives. For the environmental activist community, the progress noted above will not be viewed as sufficient, and in many cases it is not. Some activists are simply opposed to the industrial society we have created, or to corporations, or to capitalism. More moderate environmentalists are divided between those who are working with the business community to advance voluntary efforts and those more concerned with their weaknesses. The former have taken on the difficult task of convincing private sector managers that better environmental practices can be both good for the environment and good for business. Many private voluntary initiatives have been launched in partnership with NGOs that look on businesses as those with the power and resources to effect real change. Even the most hard-nosed environmental groups are willing to work with business leaders on specific, narrowly tailored projects with concrete and measurable results.

The system of private voluntary initiatives in the environmental arena suffers from a number of well-known weaknesses. The most obvious is that the initiatives still cover relatively few companies and industries, and typically only address a select number of environmental issues. The trend is positive, however, with increasing participation by a broader set of industries and an expanding menu of areas that their corporate codes address. Monitoring systems are stronger than they used to be but are often still very weak in how they measure and gather data. Information on corporate environmental practices is definitely more available today but is still quite uneven. The details of how to set up environmental accounting and auditing systems that meet international standards are still somewhat confused. Unfortunately, some firms that commit themselves to high environmental standards find that it simply raises the expectations of the public and increases the attention paid to any missteps.

Self-regulatory activity is concentrated in the industrialized countries, which already have stringent environmental regulations in place. Foreign investors often have higher standards than local industry in developing countries, but they are not always effective in transferring best practices (Garcia-Johnson 2000). Many developing country governments have only limited capacity to design and implement environmental regulations. These governments look on programs such as ISO 14000 and Responsible Care as an avenue for forcing local industry to raise its standards so that it can compete in international markets. Such programs also help developing countries respond to local demands for environmental cleanup. The chemical industry in many Asian and South American countries, where there exist strong national chemical associations, is already using these programs to improve their environmental performance (Clapp 1998). Major MNCs may be moving toward requiring that suppliers meet environmental standards in addition to technical ones, which would put pressure on developing country firms to become certified to higher standards.

The downside to this expansion of self-regulatory standards into the developing world is that many developing country governments complain they rarely have the funds to participate in international forums such as ISO, either by public or private sector representation. They often do not have access to relevant information on the standards themselves, and the certification can be expensive (Haufler 1999).[55] On one hand, many policy makers in emerging markets worry that this kind of private sector standard setting could be a disguised form of protectionism, because corporations presumably would buy only from suppliers meeting the higher standards. Those that could not meet the higher standards would be locked out of global markets. On the other hand, other policy makers feel that the future of environmental governance could be better served by private sector interests, in coordination with developing country governments, than it could be by those governments acting alone (Haas 1999, 125).

3

The Case of Labor Standards Abroad

LABOR STANDARDS are in many ways an old issue, and this has shaped the evolution of voluntary business initiatives in this area. The central labor problem is that management wants to keep the costs of production low, including the cost of labor, to reap higher profits. Marx famously pointed to the intractable differences between labor and management in an industrial era. The twentieth century has been marked by tensions between labor and management in every country. In many industrialized nations after World War II, this fundamental conflict was muted by the establishment of the welfare state and a series of compromises among the state, labor, and business leaders.[56] In the closing years of the twentieth century, the postwar bargains have fallen apart, the welfare state has been transformed, and the competition for employment now spans the globe. Dramatic changes in production technology, including the shift to an information-based economy, make it possible for corporations to increase productivity while reducing the amount of labor involved. Each major firm is part of a worldwide network of subsidiaries, partners, and suppliers. More countries are now participating in world markets than ever before, including newly industrializing countries with large pools of cheap labor. The conditions of labor in the newly industrializing countries have become a major point of contention within and across countries, dividing North and South and calling into question the sustainability of globalization.

The different ways in which governments and publics resolved, or did not resolve, worker demands in the past produced dramatically varying labor laws, unionization levels, and social welfare across countries. MNCs and their expanding networks of suppliers can use these differences to find the best combination of costs and benefits for the production of different goods and services. Many observers now question whether in doing so, these corporations entrench deep inequities among countries, sanction abusive working conditions in poor nations, and undermine the gains workers have grasped in the wealthier states. Defenders of the current system of mobile capital point to the gains foreign investment brings in terms of rising standards of living, economic growth, and modernization. The differences among countries in labor–management relations, working conditions, and wages have become a cornerstone in the debate over competitiveness, especially in the industrialized countries, as labor-intensive industries move their production facilities into developing countries in Asia and Latin America. Unions—in which membership has declined everywhere over the past decade—are struggling to identify a way to gain the benefits of globalization, such as good jobs and a better standard of living, while preserving and enhancing the bargaining power of labor in the global economy (ILO 1998).

Existing data on the disparity in wages and working conditions across countries are not very good, but even the rough information we have highlights the huge gulf between industrialized and developing countries. The ratio of average income in the richest country in the world to the poorest is about 60 to 1 today, and inequality around the world is on the rise (Birdsall 1998). Manufacturing costs in the newly industrializing economies of Asia are 36 percent of U.S. costs, while they are only 10 percent in Mexico. In 1997, the average hourly compensation of German manufacturing workers was $28.28, Japanese $18.37, and American $18.24; at the same time, the average hourly compensation of Mexican workers was only $1.75. Compensation costs in newly industrializing economies such as Taiwan, however, have increased relative to U.S. costs (U.S. Bureau of Labor Statistics 1999).[57] Variations in working conditions—from hours of work and overtime, to health and safety, to discrimination, to collective bargaining—are even more difficult to summarize. Child labor, for instance, makes up about one-third of the work force in many African countries, about 9 percent in Indonesia, 14 percent in India—but close to zero in South Korea (World Bank 1998). Practices viewed by many as unacceptable, even immoral (such as child and bonded labor), are all too common in some developing countries. The disparities of today are similar to those that emerged in the late nineteenth century, an earlier period of international economic integration, when industrialization and free trade policies wrought great changes in employment and inequality.[58]

Late twentieth-century economic liberalization stimulated business to re-organize itself to adapt to increasingly integrated markets. Approximately 200 very large firms now conduct business transnationally, with more than half their sales, employment, and investment outside of their home countries.[59] They invest primarily in the industrialized countries but increasingly look to the newly emerging markets for high returns and potential new consumers. There are more than 53,000 TNCs with about 450,000 affiliates today (UNCTAD 2000). Multinational firms are the world's largest employers, and they determine the wages and working conditions of employees located in a multiplicity of national jurisdictions. The largest private sector employer in the world is Wal-Mart, with approximately 1,140,000 employees, which is greater than the population of many small nations such as Estonia or Gabon (Fortune 2000).[60] The number of truly transnational firms is still small, but many small- and medium-sized companies now have at least some international operations (UNCTAD 2000).

At the same time as recent high-profile mergers and acquisitions such as Daimler Chrysler and AOL Time Warner highlight the growing size of corporations and concentration of markets, many firms are also going the opposite route (sometimes simultaneously). Many companies now decentralize the organization of production to become "network" organizations. The term *network corporation* has become a buzzword to describe the ways in which one firm links with other firms in joint ventures, strategic alliances, partnerships, supplier relationships, and licensing agreements that blur the boundaries of the firm. For example, General Motors, one of the largest companies in the world, has a network of over 30,000 individual suppliers; it manufactures in over 50 countries and has a presence in about 200 countries; and it has over 260 major subsidiaries, joint venture partners, and affiliates (General Motors 2000).

Many companies now produce goods by farming out portions of the production process to subcontractors—and to their subcontractors and sub-subcontractors, sometimes numbering in the thousands. Disney alone has over 6,000 subcontractors for its various products. Long supply chains are particularly common in the sectors in which there is the most criticism of labor standards: textiles, apparel, footwear, toys, and sporting goods. The result of this complex outsourcing is that name-brand companies sell goods made by people who are not direct employees. Nike, for instance, does not own factories but rather contracts with factories around the world to supply the products it designs and puts its logo on. This new organization of production makes it extremely difficult for labor to maintain a balance of power with management, especially because a national union often does not have the ability to take effective action against the overseas buyers. Foreign corporations have a huge influence on working conditions in these countries, even without owning directly any production facilities.

In *Has Globalization Gone Too Far?* Dani Rodrik analyzes how reduced barriers to trade and investment highlight the asymmetry between groups that can cross international borders and those that cannot (that is, owners of capital, highly skilled workers, and professionals as compared to the unskilled, semi-skilled, and even middle managers). "As the technology for manufactured goods becomes standardized and diffused internationally, nations with very different sets of values, norms, institutions, and collective preferences begin to compete head on in markets for similar goods" (Rodrik 1997). Governments may find it harder to supply social welfare benefits, and unions may find it harder to bargain for higher wages and better working conditions (Rodrik 1997; Kyloh 1998). Owners and managers argue in response that their competitiveness relies on their access to a flexible global workforce (Kapstein 1999). Among developing countries, where social welfare programs are weak to nonexistent and unions are often illegal, there is intense competition to attract foreign investors and labor-intensive employment.

Three traditional means for redressing poor working conditions are, in the eyes of many critics, inadequate to meet the needs of labor in a period of rapid economic globalization. First, the idea that governments will protect workers through appropriate legislation and enforcement is unrealistic in many developing countries. Even with the best will in the world, the political infrastructure may not be in place to ensure that working conditions meet established standards. And, in many cases, the will is also missing. Indeed, some governments deliberately pursue policies that lead to lower labor standards for a variety of reasons—repression of labor unrest, desire to attract foreign investment, policies that favor one group over another, and resistance by industrial elites. However, we cannot say this is true everywhere, and in fact, wages and working conditions have improved in some of the newly industrialized countries. In general, the most problematic countries for labor rights, such as China or Vietnam, are the ones that are fairly impervious to political demands for change, especially if made by foreign governments or activists.

Historically the most potent tools in the hands of labor have been unionization and collective bargaining. Many of the countries where the conditions of work have become an international issue are countries where unions are either outlawed or suppressed, where collective bargaining is uncommon, and where the power of labor as a political force is weak. Major international labor organizations—such as the International Confederation of Free Trade Unions (ICFTU) and the American Federation of Labor and the Congress of Industrial Organizations (AFL-CIO), and others—have tried to promote and support labor organizers abroad, but the political barriers to success are high.

Finally, the third means toward raising worldwide labor standards is through international economic organizations, such as the ILO. The ILO has great, but as yet unrealized, potential to be a bulwark against the exploitation of workers.[61] In recent years, the role of the ILO has been revitalized with the reaffirmation and acceptance of the fundamental or core principles of the ILO. At the same time, many labor activists are pressing for labor issues to be incorporated into other more powerful organizations, such as the World Trade Organization.

The weaknesses, real and perceived, of these three avenues for the improvement of working conditions have helped propel corporate behavior into the forefront of debates. If states are unwilling or unable to act, if labor is unorganized, and if international organizations are weak, then some new alternative must be devised. The last actor standing, the one with the most direct and immediate control over the lives of workers, is of course the private sector. The rise of the MNC means that the lives of workers often are deeply influenced by decisions made by foreigners. Business leaders now must manage their relations with home and host governments, local business partners, and workers at home and abroad, which forces them to engage in an increasingly complex form of international diplomacy (Stopford and

Strange 1991). The following section discusses the background and development of codes of conduct and social auditing as measures of industry self-regulation. Then the next section discusses how risk, reputation, and learning all influenced the evolution of the trends we see. And the final section looks at important issues of consensus, enforcement, and participation in the design and implementation of industry self-regulation.

Codes of Conduct, Ethical Trade, and Monitoring Programs

Major human rights groups put labor on the international agenda by the late 1980s and early 1990s. Human Rights Watch, Amnesty International, the International Labor Rights Fund, plus unions, consumer groups, churches, and social justice campaigners forcefully began to pressure governments around the world to address—and redress—the exploitative conditions found in many developing countries. They focused on an array of related issues: unsafe and unhealthy working conditions, extremely long working hours, exploitation of child labor, discrimination against women or particular ethnic groups, the use of forced labor, the suppression of freedom of association and collective bargaining, and the lack of a "living wage."[62] They pointed in particular to what they saw as the inevitable results of intense economic competition in labor-intensive industries such as apparel, footwear, toys, and sports equipment. The broader human rights activist networks took up the cause of labor.

The protests against working conditions abroad emerged hand-in-hand with profoundly divisive debates over economic liberalization and the emergence of an antiglobalization coalition that spanned international borders. In the United States, the unions argued against NAFTA and a new round of GATT negotiations partly by pointing out the low wages and miserable working conditions in developing countries. Critics depicted the unions as cynically trying to protect their members from competition from low-wage labor abroad, without a genuine concern for workers in other countries.

Many local activists in the 1980s and 1990s successfully persuaded state and local governments in the United States and Europe to adopt sanctions against countries that violate minimum labor standards, as defined by the ILO. The issue of sanctions riled the business community, especially in the United States, where they complained that the proliferation of sanctions was difficult to administer, made long-range planning impossible, and generally created too many problems for them in doing business abroad. In the United States, the reauthorization of most-favored-nation treatment for China was used each year to publicize Chinese labor and human rights policy and put pressure on Congress to authorize sanctions.

The business community woke up to the increasing power of this labor activism through a number of high profile cases. Activists accused television personality Kathie Lee Gifford of complicity in sweatshop labor because she endorsed a line of clothing for Wal-Mart. Much of this clothing was stitched in factories in Honduras that employed children in twenty-hour workdays. In recent years, critical attacks on Nike have made it the poster child for the sweatshop issue, and its profits and market share have been declining.[63] In 1996, CBS reported on sweatshop conditions in a factory in Vietnam that supplied Nike products. Within a year, a new NGO, Vietnam Labor Watch, formed to monitor Nike's actions publicly. The "campaign of embarrassment" against retail giants and media personalities brought home to consumers the work conditions in the places where imported clothing was made (Varley 1998). A new anti-sweatshop movement began to gain headway among activists, consumers, and especially students in the United States, Canada, and Australia. Campus activism emerged as a significant factor in the late 1990s, as students across the United States demanded that university logo goods be certified as "sweatshop-free."

Many firms strongly resisted outside demands, refusing to provide information about working conditions and subcontractor operations, rejecting any community engagement, opposing unions and collective bargaining, and accepting the poor living conditions in developing countries. But others have pursued a more accommodationist policy, responding to new political pressures by launching voluntary initiatives addressing labor conditions at home and abroad. Their efforts fall into three basic categories: individual corporate initiatives, such as a corporate code of conduct; group initiatives, either within an industry sector or in partnership with public interest groups; and acceptance of third-party oversight. Those three categories reflect the evolution of the self-regulatory movement on labor issues, as corporations have moved from weak individual codes to ever stronger collective public commitments.

Initially, a number of corporations simply handed down a new corporate code of conduct developed by top management or by an outside consultant. These codes would lay out high-minded principles for ethical behavior and establish a commitment to treating workers fairly. They were often empty statements of sentiment suitable for public consumption and marketing purposes. The codes languished at headquarters and never were publicized widely within the corporation, or else they were trotted out for public consumption to burnish the image of the company when necessary. Workers often knew little or nothing about them—especially workers in foreign factories looking at statements written in English. The weaknesses of these codes gave them a bad reputation.

Nike unveiled a corporate code of conduct in 1992 but suffered unrelenting criticism because the code's provisions and implementation were so weak. Nike does not own factories abroad but instead depends on an extensive network of global suppliers. At first, Nike defended itself by arguing that it could not be responsible for the actions of its suppliers. The activists, however, mobilized a significant amount of negative media attention and organized a lawsuit in U.S. courts against Nike for falsely advertising that its products were not made in sweatshop conditions. Nike hired the well-respected Andrew Young to visit and audit suppliers in Vietnam; the resulting relatively positive report garnered scathing criticism. Nike then hired the accountants Ernst and Young to do a more thorough audit, but this too met with little respect. Meanwhile, Nike did implement new policies and pressured its suppliers to raise wages in Vietnam and improve their facilities. As one critic pointed out, "They saw some pretty scary marketing research that 12-year-old girls in focus groups were talking about these labour abuses" (Harverson 1999).

Many other firms also began to develop codes of conduct in the 1990s for the treatment of labor abroad. A number of them tried to ensure the codes were properly implemented by establishing management procedures within the corporations, as part of a wider human relations–personnel function within the firm. These companies set up systems to encourage workers to report violations (often setting up a toll-free number for such reports), translated all documents into the native language of the workers, and monitored their own compliance. These codes applied primarily to direct employees.

Levi Strauss & Co. developed and implemented Global Sourcing and Operating Guidelines, which rest fundamentally on its Business Partner Terms of Engagement. This became a model for codes that regulate the behavior of suppliers and subcontractors. The document is a set of guiding principles for choosing business partners and identifying potential problems in advance. The Levi's code states that contractors are expected to be ethical, to be law-abiding, and to meet employment standards. These employment standards include: minimum wages or prevailing wages, setting reasonable working hours not to exceed 60 hours per week, not using child labor less than fourteen years old or prison or forced labor, maintaining a safe and healthy work environment, and not discriminating among employees or using punishment or coercion to discipline workers. Levi's also produces country risk assessments to understand how likely violations might be in different cultural settings. Most important, top management is committed to these principles. For instance, Levi's at one time withdrew its business from China when it could not be sure these standards could be met.

Reebok, seeing the writing on the wall after the media tarring of Nike, chose to improve its practices preemptively. Reebok instituted a policy of refusing to buy soccer balls from factories using child labor. Instead of going it alone, however, it obtained support first from the World Federation of Sporting Goods Industries and the U.S. Sporting Goods Manufacturers Association. These collective commitments can create stronger incentives, for buyer and seller alike. In this case, Reebok felt reassured that other manufacturers would be less likely to undercut it in this market. Sellers, faced with a collective refusal to buy soccer balls made by children, had to change their practices.

At the same time as the corporate code "movement" advanced, many other groups began to promote the adoption by companies of various codes. Labor advocates, unions, governments, and international organizations all began experimenting with cooperative approaches to regulation. In these cases, the standards and systems of implementation are designed in concert, but the final result is a voluntary initiative and not new regulation. Human rights organizations and coalitions developed their own codes for corporations to adopt. By the mid-1990s, Amnesty International, the Interfaith Center on Corporate Responsibility, the Clean Clothes Campaign in Europe, and others all had labor codes for international operations that they asked businesses to adopt.

New center-left political administrations in the United Kingdom, United States, and Canada saw opportunity in the growing number of corporate codes. In North America, this attention took root particularly with the debate over the NAFTA. Activists wanted to make the further opening of national markets conditional on governments enforcing particular labor standards. They succeeded in persuading the U.S. government to incorporate labor (and environment) side agreements into the NAFTA in 1994. This was the first time a major trade agreement directly addressed labor issues (Wise 1998). The Clinton administration wanted to conclude NAFTA without alienating labor, but the adamant opposition of AFL-CIO to the agreement made it a hard-fought political battle.

In 1995, the Canadian media focused for a brief time on a thirteen-year-old Canadian boy who created the NGO Free the Children. He linked it via the Internet with Asian-based NGOs such as Child Workers in Asia and developed a common platform with them. He spoke to labor unions, was covered by the Canadian and international media, and raised a significant sum of money to travel to Asia to visit child workers in slums, factories, and brothels. After initial resistance, he eventually was able to meet with the Prime Minister Jean Chretien to tell him that Canada must have a policy in which trade is linked to labor standards (English 2000, 1).[64] Canadian business remained staunchly opposed to linking trade and labor, and both the government and industry representatives began to look at industry self-regulation codes as one way to address the labor standards debate.

The Canadian, U.S., and British governments all sought ways to use corporate voluntary self-regulation to deal with the increasingly contentious issue of sweatshop labor in developing countries. In 1995 the Clinton administration announced its Model Business Principles for U.S. firms to adopt into their own corporate codes. It urged corporations to take responsibility voluntarily for the labor standards of suppliers and partners abroad. Shortly afterward, the U.S. Secretary of Labor Robert Reich launched a "No Sweat" campaign against sweatshop labor at home and abroad. The Model Business Principles were never widely adopted, however, in part because business viewed them as too much a product of government.

Clinton administration officials then turned to a more ambitious program, facilitating negotiations between business and its critics. It helped launch the Apparel Industry Partnership (AIP), consisting of eighteen garment makers and labor and human rights groups. The AIP began meeting in 1996 to develop basic labor standards to govern factories and suppliers in the textile, apparel, and footwear industries.[65] The U.S. government had no direct vote on the outcome of negotiations among these groups but helped bring the participants together. The outcome of the negotiations under the AIP would be developed through a multiparty process with representatives from a range of interested groups and not just business alone. This gave them much greater potential to gain public legitimacy than purely company-sponsored plans.

The negotiations lasted for three years and almost broke down completely at one point. The participants engaged in often contentious debate over the appropriate set of standards and how to implement them. The most divisive issues concerned the design of a monitoring system, unionization, and especially the issue of a living wage. Some original members of the AIP, including the Union of Needletrades, Industrial, and Textile Employees (UNITE), withdrew from the process. After UNITE withdrew, a handful of major corporate participants, including Nike, Liz Claiborne, Phillips Van Heusen, and Reebok, stayed in and finally agreed to some basic principles. They decided to establish an independent Fair Labor Association (FLA), a private entity split between corporate and human rights/labor representatives. The FLA would accredit auditors to certify company compliance with the agreed standards. The FLA officially began to operate in late 1999, and it is still too early to determine its ultimate impact.

In part as a response to the negotiations in the AIP, the American Apparel Manufacturers Association (AAMA) developed its own industry guidelines for its member companies. These Worldwide Responsible Apparel Production (WRAP) Principles and Certification Program are intended to help companies police their factories and suppliers. Members of the AAMA had been targets of high-profile attacks; they joined the AAMA because the AIP at times seemed either on the verge of collapse, or about to include what they viewed as unreasonable standards. The AAMA ensured that the WRAP includes many fundamental labor rights but excludes contentious elements such as freedom of association and collective bargaining. Each company that signs on to the WRAP makes a commitment to have its factories independently inspected.

The British government under Tony Blair also launched an initiative designed to harness corporate voluntary action to "ethical" foreign policy goals. The Blair government created what it called the Ethical Trading Initiative (ETI) in January 1998. The ETI is a program that includes equal representation by business, workers organizations, and NGOs. It aims to develop and encourage voluntary adoption of a set of standards and monitoring and auditing methods for the apparel industry. Unlike in the United States, a fairly large number of British corporations, nonprofits, and unions have signed on to it.

Other voluntary initiatives focused on specific industries, such as the carpet industry in India, soccer ball manufacturing in Pakistan, and others. For instance, the Confederation of British Industry, UN Children's Fund (UNICEF), and the British government launched a combined campaign against child labor. Carpet industry officials in India negotiated with child and labor activists and the UNICEF to eliminate child labor in the industry, largely due to pressure from German consumer groups. They developed the Rugmark program, which monitors factory worksheets and certifies carpets are made without child labor. The negotiations addressed one of the most difficult issues —the future of the children themselves, given the poverty of their families. The Rugmark program includes funding to place former child workers in school programs and replace their wages with aid. The ILO initiated a similar program in 1996 with soccer ball manufacturers and exporters in Pakistan. In both cases, the voluntary program by industry involved an explicit commitment by governments and international organizations to treat the elimination of child labor in part as a development aid issue.

One of the most significant developments in the area of industry self-regulation was not an actual corporate or industry code or standards program. In 1998, the Council on Economic Priorities (CEP), a nonprofit association with a long history of promoting corporate social responsibility, launched an effort to develop social accounting standards. The system, modeled on the ISO standard-setting process, is called SA 8000. CEP developed it with the input of retail associations, Amnesty International, SGS International Certification Services, Reebok, the International Textile Workers Union, and others. SA 8000 is a set of verifiable standards that includes child labor, forced or slave labor, worker safety, and freedom of association. Unlike ISO 14000, the SA 8000 standards are both process and performance standards. Social Accountability International (SAI) administers the standards and trains and certifies individuals to conduct social audits. Companies hire SAI-certified auditors who assess whether or not the firm can be certified as meeting SA 8000 standards. The incentives for businesses to adopt SA 8000 are the reputation effects of certification and the inclusion in socially screened mutual funds. Neil Kearney, Secretary-General of the International Textile, Garment, and Leather Workers Federation, joined the Board of the SA 8000. He argues that it is impractical to construct codes and monitoring systems industry by industry and that professional certification firms would be an improvement over the current alternatives (English 2000, 12).[66]

The AIP, WRAP, Rugmark, and other programs were developed about the same time as international pressure mounted to link trade and labor in international negotiations. By the end of the 1990s, unions, labor activists, and human rights organizations pressed national governments from around the world to put labor standards on the agenda of the next round of global trade negotiations under the WTO. Representatives to the WTO steadfastly refused to admit any link between free trade negotiations and labor standards until its ministerial meeting in Singapore in 1997. There, WTO leaders acknowledged a link between trade and labor but reaffirmed the role of the ILO as the competent body to handle labor issues. The new Secretary-General of the ILO, Juan Samovia, saw an opportunity to reinvigorate the organization. After only one year of discussion, in 1998 the ILO declared that eight of the ILO conventions constituted fundamental principles for rights at work, and the membership voted to make them binding on all members, whether or not each nation formally adopted the relevant conventions.[67] In 1999, the ILO adopted a new convention against the worst forms of abusive child labor, which came into force in November 2000.[68] In contrast, in late 2000, the members of the WTO met in Seattle to launch a new round of trade negotiations, but the launch was scuttled by deep divisions among governments about whether to continue and by massive protests from a wide variety of pressure groups opposed to globalization.

In concert with activism against globalization, many students mobilized against sweatshops by the end of the late 1990s. The leadership of major U.S. universities reacted swiftly by adopting guidelines for university logo-wear. Recently, five universities worked with Business for Social Responsibility, the Investor Responsibility Research Center, and a consultant to gather information about working conditions in countries that manufacture university logo apparel.[69] They concluded that working conditions are poor, corporate codes and monitoring are too weak, and the proliferation of codes and monitoring efforts does not lead to greater compliance (Independent University Initiative 2000). Many of the university leaders do not want to repeat the stonewalling of students that characterized the campus anti-apartheid movement of a decade earlier. The students demanded that the universities adopt a monitoring system. Most universities chose the Fair Labor Association, although many of the student anti-sweatshop activists supported a new alternative, the Worker Rights Consortium. At about the same time, the Reverend Leon Sullivan also launched the new Global Sullivan Principles, a code of corporate conduct promoting human rights, economic justice, racial and gender equality, and a healthy environment.

In early 1999, keeping up the pressure on corporations, activists filed a lawsuit against Wal-Mart, The Gap, The Limited, Sears, Dayton-Hudson, and others. It accused them of a "racketeering conspiracy" to use indentured labor to produce clothing in Saipan. Two class-action lawsuits were filed on behalf of Saipan workers, and a third was brought by four labor and human rights groups—Sweatshop Watch, Global Exchange, Asian Law Caucus, and UNITE.[70] The goal is to convince U.S. corporations to cut off their contracts with Saipan factories or enforce higher standards on them. Litigation as a tactic for NGOs depends on a court system that allows lawsuits for actions taken abroad. In the United States, the Alien Tort Claims Act allows such lawsuits, and they are increasingly being brought against companies accused of labor abuses.

Throughout the 1990s, new sources of pressure against corporations emerged in the rapidly growing financial markets. Labor groups, taking a page from the book of anti-apartheid activists, took advantage of the widening pool of investors and consumers who are willing to use their investment money to support a cause. A small but growing group of U.S., British, and Japanese mutual funds began to screen for socially responsible companies and included labor standards as one of their screens. Large institutional investors, serving thousands of individual investors, such as TIAA-CREF in the United States, began to offer socially screened alternatives. A number of religious groups, unions, and NGOs submitted resolutions to shareholders at annual meetings, proposing for instance that company management should refuse to do business in countries with abusive labor practices. In the United States, the Investor Responsibility Resource Center and the Interfaith Center for Corporate Responsibility both have promoted shareholder activism.

Most resolutions fail to receive enough votes to become policy. But even failed shareholder resolutions affect management, increasing their perceived vulnerability to outside pressures. In April 1999, Disney committed to auditing the labor practices of 15,000 of its overseas subcontractors after being pressured to do so by shareholders, even though those activists were not successful at passing a shareholder resolution on this issue. Disney management clearly perceived a threat that its sales could drop sharply if consumers believed Disney was not upholding high standards. Mattel, Inc. also feared for its reputation. In response, Mattel developed its own set of supplier guidelines. It also asked an independent group to establish a global monitoring system to make sure that its standards would be implemented. Mattel went so far as to make its first report public in spring 2000. The first report revealed both strengths and weaknesses in compliance by suppliers, and Mattel committed itself to rectifying any problems it found.

The Canadian government, under pressure for not doing enough on international labor issues, closely watched what was happening in the United States and Great Britain. Simon Zadek, a key player in British initiatives, visited Canada often to speak to business and government representatives. Canadian officials followed the negotiations over the U.S. AIP to draw lessons about how this issue might play out in their country, and what role voluntary self-regulation could play. Promotion of corporate codes appeared to be a way to further the government's commitment to human security as the keynote of its foreign policy. In 1998 the Canadian government issued a handbook for business on codes of conduct, declaring codes a supplement and even an alternative to traditional regulatory approaches (Government of Canada 1998).

Following the publication of the handbook, government officials also facilitated meetings between business and NGOs throughout 1999 to develop a consensus code of conduct for Canadian business. The Canadian Manufacturers of Canada, under fire from human rights and labor activists, actually invited the government to help.[71] Labor and NGO representatives formed a coalition called the Ethical Trading Action Group (ETAG) to negotiate with business and government. The working group on these codes included a representative from UNITE, a union that had participated in and then withdrew from the U.S. AIP.[72] Industry associations that had already been considering corporate codes joined in these government-sponsored efforts, including the Canadian Chamber of Commerce, the Retail Council of Canada, and the Alliance of Manufacturers and Exporters. The Canadian Partnership for Ethical Trading (CPET), as it came to be called, spent a year negotiating a Canadian code of conduct.

The negotiations over this Canadian code ran into many conflicts and tensions among business and NGO representatives, as was to be expected. Business was concerned about increased costs at a time when the Canadian retail industry had weakened. They worried about legal liability in foreign countries if the code contradicted foreign laws. They also wanted a federal government presence in the process. The labor and civil society representatives had a detailed list of preferences, many drawn directly from ILO conventions, the Ethical Trading Initiative, the AIP, and other initiatives. They worried, however, that a too-close partnership with business could harm their reputation with their members.[73] Both sides recognized a need to educate their respective constituencies to bring them on board.[74] The government appointed a facilitator and did not take direct part in the negotiations. This reflected ambivalence within the government as trade officials worried over protectionism, and foreign affairs officials worried that other countries were going further faster in promoting ethical business practices. The CPET negotiations broke down in spring 2000, although industry representatives subsequently made a commitment to develop their own codes. ETAG later complained that the Canadian government did not provide sufficient financial support for the process and that it should have put more pressure on industry in the negotiations (English 2000, 16).

By summer 2000, efforts to link worker rights with trade sanctions in global and regional institutions had met with limited success. The WTO now does a better job of engaging with civil society organizations, and international labor organizations continue to be active (Wilkinson and Hughes 2000, 260). There has been some softening of the position of pro-labor groups from a preference for punitive enforcement (which looked like protectionism and neo-imperialism) to a focus on promoting core labor standards that would give workers the means to claim an equitable share of the benefits of freer trade (Wilkinson and Hughes 2000, 262). Union groups such as the ICFTU support core labor standards within a regional strategy. Social clauses have been inserted into the EU and NAFTA, are being discussed in the Latin American Mercosur, and have been proposed in the Southern African Development Community and Asia Pacific Economic Cooperation forum (APEC).

Risk, Reputation, and Learning

Clearly, the pressures facing business on labor issues reached a peak in the mid-1990s. The threat of government regulation or strong international action to link trade and labor were real possibilities, and in NAFTA that link was made concretely for the first time. Activists had become increasingly adept at using diverse and innovative tools to press their cause against high-profile corporations, using shareholder activism and litigation in concert with media attention, boycotts, and protests. Human rights groups, unions, anti-globalization activists, religious groups, and others successfully mobilized over the sweatshop issue. They became increasingly successful at lobbying policy makers in Europe and North America to take action on labor conditions abroad. Many business leaders figured that the political risks of inaction outweighed the perceived cost of action.

The economic risks facing the major buyers of goods produced abroad are also very high. Global competition to produce low-cost, labor-intensive goods such as apparel and footwear is fierce, among both major buyers and the multitude of suppliers. The buyers who are most often accused of condoning sweatshop labor, such as Nike, are global companies locked in combat for market share. The suppliers compete among themselves to supply the major companies, with factories in Vietnam competing with those in Guatemala. This makes it extremely difficult for management to contemplate increasing the amount they pay in labor costs, unless it is done collectively within an industry or imposed more broadly by governments. At the same time, given the extremely low living standards in many countries, raising wages or improving working conditions even marginally would make little difference in the overall cost of the product but would have a great impact on workers. Many of the demands regarding worker rights, such as forbidding discrimination, do not entail direct economic costs. The latter runs into primarily cultural barriers, not economic ones.

Activist campaigns are most effective against highly visible brand names, such as Starbucks and Toys R Us, and brands that use well-known personalities such as Kathie Lee Gifford to put a face to the "faceless" corporation. Activists use the spotlight of public opinion to highlight corporate abuses and encourage change (Spar 1998). One well-timed exposé in the media can ruin years of building a brand-name reputation. Companies with a global brand name that sell directly to consumers put a high value on their reputation. For companies such as Disney or Mattel, the images in the media of children in foreign countries working twenty-hour days to make toys for children in wealthy countries can be devastating.

One of the most telling aspects of the international debate over labor standards and the role of the private sector is the different kinds of learning (and not learning) taking place. The Canadian effort to negotiate a Canadian corporate code demonstrates a case of political learning. The participants in CPET included representatives of the union UNITE, which had had a negative experience from its participation in the AIP in the United States. The Canadian government tried to forestall the kinds of divisions that led UNITE and others to withdraw from the AIP. The unions and NGOs participating in CPET presented a proposal that drew from many earlier efforts they had engaged in or studied in the United States and United Kingdom, but also added elements drawn from their representatives' experience at the ILO. Both business and labor explicitly organized or participated in educational processes intended to promote industry voluntary self-regulation. Representatives of apparel and shoe manufacturers regularly met with government officials, who briefed them on relevant trends abroad. The Canadian Retail Council sponsored a series of workshops on corporate social responsibility—although it is not clear what message these workshops ultimately conveyed (English 2000, 11).

Businesses also learned in different ways about the significance of labor issues and corporate social responsibility. High-profile activist campaigns directed against name-brand manufacturers taught them the cost of being targeted. Once Nike had been chosen as a target by activists, Reebok executives realized their company would be next in line for attention, and they began to develop stricter corporate policies on sweatshop issues. Unfortunately, some businesses learned the "wrong" lesson from this. When Nike, Reebok, and Levi Strauss suffered from critical attention *after* they adopted a code of conduct, some business leaders decided it was safer to stay out of the public eye. In general, business leaders have been unresponsive to the argument that even the lowest level, unskilled, or semi-skilled workers will be more productive if they are treated well. When firms do respond and implement self-regulatory programs, they each define good treatment differently, and there is relatively little consensus over the standards to promote abroad.

Few business groups are dedicated to educating the business community about the value of upholding high standards for labor. Business for Social Responsibility and the Prince of Wales Business Leaders Forum promote corporate social responsibility in general, but business leaders have no interest in establishing business organizations specifically devoted to promoting higher standards for workers. The AAMA might be one exception, but it is narrowly focused on one industry—apparel—and was not initially created to promote labor standards. The lack of business organizations whose sole purpose is to raise international labor standards is a result of the long history of antagonism between labor and management. Labor issues have traditionally been addressed at the national level, in well developed systems of labor–management relations, often involving an extensive legal framework for collective bargaining. In addition, business interests are directly represented in the ILO. Therefore, there is little incentive for business to develop new organizations—in contrast to the environmental case.

Some companies now seek out partnerships with NGOs and governments instead of going it alone. Others find the process of developing their own corporate code to be a valuable organizational exercise. The internal process of developing a code can be an educational effort that imparts values throughout the organization and gives management more ownership of the policy. The substance of such codes reflects the problems and issues particular to that company, to its own suppliers and contractors, and to the specific locales in which it operates. Because this system is closed to outside scrutiny, however, many issues do not get raised, and those outside the organization may not view the end result as legitimate.

Consensus, Enforcement, and Accountability

Industry self-regulatory initiatives, from single-firm corporate codes to industry association standards to broader partnerships with other actors, all suffer from three perceived significant weaknesses: disagreement over the standards, lack of strict enforcement mechanisms, and no well-defined way to hold companies accountable. Such weaknesses lead labor advocates, unions, and human rights groups to view self-regulation with a large degree of skepticism. As many companies have learned, adopting a corporate code or even some more proactive program of improvement for labor does not always relieve the pressure from outside to institute even further improvements.

There is some disagreement, however, among the many stakeholders over whether these weaknesses truly exist. For instance, many people argue that there is broad consensus over labor standards. They point to ILO conventions negotiated among representatives of labor, employers, and governments. They argue that the recently revised OECD Guidelines on Multinational Enterprises represent international consensus. The private sector in contrast argues that these guidelines are directed more toward governments than companies. More important, they point out that these broad guidelines often conflict with law, regulation, and culture in specific national circumstances. A company dedicated to promoting women into management positions will simply not be able to do so effectively in Saudi Arabia.

Companies with suppliers in China do not know how to promote freedom of association in a country in which it is outlawed. Facing these challenges, many companies essentially pick and choose which particular standard to apply in each situation. For instance, most corporate codes say nothing about unions and collective bargaining, which the ILO and unions view as fundamental to all other worker rights.

Critics accuse industry of choosing the self-regulatory programs that favor their interests, and not those of the workers. For instance, unions point to freedom of association and a living wage as the key to improving the lives of workers, and in the United States they were willing to walk out on the AIP over these issues. However, workers in developing countries do not always have the same perspective as workers and activists in industrialized countries. They often view foreign subsidiaries and suppliers to world markets as their best hope for improving their living conditions. All of this points to a lack of real consensus on standards, wages, and rights. Governments, employers, workers, and activists may aspire to all the standards embodied in international agreements, but profound differences exist on the ground.

Moreover, some improvements for workers are more within the purview of corporations than others. A firm can raise wages or improve health and safety in a factory relatively easily, but it cannot easily change a political system that forbids some of the fundamental rights enumerated in international agreements. Corporate codes can be a tool to facilitate some kinds of improvements, but there are limits on what they can do. In general, foreign investment improves the lot of working people, and workers in foreign subsidiaries or in factories that supply world markets generally have better wages and working conditions than local firms. Corporate codes can be used to further improve overseas operations, especially when they are extended beyond the firm to cover suppliers. This has the potential to set up a positive dynamic to create real change.

One of the big developments in industry self-regulation over time has been the evolution of increasingly sophisticated systems of monitoring and compliance. These do not amount to strong enforcement, as with government regulations, but they can be viewed as a form of "soft law." Initially, most of these systems were internal to the corporation, and the companies essentially certified or audited their own behavior. For many, even this step was a big one—never before had they attempted to gather corporatewide information on a broad range of labor issues. As in any large bureaucracy, the leaders often found that standards at the top had not filtered down to the bottom. Many corporations now outsource this function to accounting and auditing firms, which see a growing market in global social accounting and auditing. These in-house assessments are rarely, if ever, made public and are often dismissed by critics, as in the case of Nike audits.[75]

In the past few years, Levi Strauss, Mattel, Disney, and others have developed new standards that both the companies and their suppliers —sometimes thousands of suppliers—must meet. This requires a much more sophisticated and complicated system of monitoring, one that many companies are reluctant to undertake. Guidelines for supplier relations require the company to collect information that is extremely difficult to obtain. A company would need to hire staff to evaluate and audit factories, one by one, to see whether they complied with the standards. The evaluations themselves can be extremely difficult, since most local managers are not forthcoming about practices such as paying below-minimum wages or using child labor. As more buyers adopt supplier codes, a new problem has emerged: because individual factories manufacture goods for different buyers, they are suddenly finding that they must comply with more than one set of standards.

A handful of firms now also accept external monitoring. External monitors can include traditional auditors and accountants who make their reports public or who certify the company to a particular set of standards. The AIP established its own independent monitoring organization, the FLA, which evaluates how well particular factories meet the AIP standards. Mattel funded an independent auditing group, MIMCO, to conduct thorough reviews of working conditions at its supplier factories. And of course, the SA 8000 social auditing and certification process has great potential for creating uniform measures of comparability and benchmarking of factories and firms.[76] Once SA 8000 has been in place and utilized by a broad range of firms in different countries over time, then more data on actual trends in corporate social performance will be available. One of the problems in monitoring working conditions or human rights has been to move beyond the anecdotal, according to Eileen Kohl Kaufman of SAI (personal communication).

These monitoring systems, while an advance in terms of ensuring compliance, are still quite controversial. For instance, SAI has been careful to state that they do not intend SA 8000 to impose standards on developing countries, even though that is in fact the probable result. They also have chosen to certify firms on only a handful of standards drawn from the ILO Fundamental Rights at Work, thus limiting its scope. Critics outside the business community complain that the standards only address what is measurable, that they are applied to entire companies instead of separate facilities, and that they do little to deal with the problem of overseas suppliers. Those same criticisms apply to other monitoring efforts as well.

Unfortunately, even the best-designed monitoring systems rely on something that most corporations simply do not have: good information systems that provide accurate data on how well the company does or does not meet particular standards. Existing accounting procedures and record keeping systems are not designed to provide the kind of data that are needed for effective monitoring. Observers debate the quality of the information gathered in social audits and disagree over their interpretation. For instance, in an audit, the company paperwork on wages may not be accurate (and in fact can be downright fraudulent). Workers may be asked whether they are paid the minimum wage, and some may say what their managers want them to say, while others may say what they think the auditor wants to hear. Although audits represent a step forward from simple codes to something more substantive, there are still a number of challenges to make them work effectively.

Finally, one of the remaining concerns of those suspicious of industry self-regulation is accountability. Critics see self-regulatory processes as inherently illegitimate, because the companies essentially are making up their own rules. Once the rules are developed, the company determines its own degree of compliance. There are, however, certain mechanisms of accountability in place in some voluntary initiatives. MNCs that adopt a corporate code often establish a system of accountability within the corporate organization, establishing particular positions and people who are responsible for implementing corporate policy. Increasingly, as described above, companies conduct internal and external auditing of their performance. Public reporting of the results is a form of accountability. In addition, companies that do not work alone but in cooperation with other companies, NGOs, and governments can be held accountable by those partners. More companies today adopt these practices than did ten years ago. At the same time, however, the majority of companies with business overseas do not self-regulate their own or their suppliers' labor standards, and relatively few subject themselves to external monitoring or certification programs.

––––––––––

INDUSTRY SELF-REGULATION in the area of worker rights has great potential to improve the lives of many people living in developing countries. To date, however, these codes of conduct have not lived up to their claims. The companies that are most prominently pushing their corporate codes of conduct have been accused of laxness in implementing their own policies. Individual companies have struggled to develop a means of applying their standards not just to their own organizations, but also to suppliers and the suppliers to the suppliers. In some political and economic contexts, there simply is no way for a company to be absolutely sure that its code is being upheld 100 percent. After a series of reports on poor working conditions in Asian subcontractor factories was released, a number of activist groups combined to launch a Boycott Nike Campaign in 1999. Levi Strauss, which was a leader in developing its Global Sourcing Guidelines, also has been a target of critical reports and claims that it has not fully implemented the excellent guidelines it established.[77]

Corporate codes are popular in only a few specific sectors—apparel, textile, footwear, toy, sporting goods, and carpet industries. The structure of supplier relations means that only a handful of countries are touched by the global codes, with Asian countries such as Vietnam, China, Indonesia, and Bangladesh common sourcing sites. Industry self-regulation is not as common or publicly visible in other industries or other countries. It is no surprise that labor codes are most common in labor-intensive industries and those that employ extensive outsourcing.[78] The actual content of industry codes typically addresses only the issues that are in the public eye, with new ones added to the list as attention is paid to them. Oftentimes, human rights and labor advocacy groups campaign on a particular issue, which then shows up in corporate codes. The transnational activists set the agenda, which may or may not be the particular agenda that developing country workers themselves would choose. In recent years the hot topic has been child labor. Individual governments launched campaigns against child labor, and the ILO has established an ambitious program to eradicate it. The business community has also gotten involved with these efforts, as with the Rugmark program.

Not surprisingly, few corporate codes commit the company to uphold freedom of association and the right of workers to organize into unions and bargain collectively. It is simply impractical to promise this in countries where both are outlawed by the political regime, such as in China. Some unions, such as the ICFTU, are cautiously supportive of some voluntary initiatives. Others are deeply concerned that companies will use their self-regulatory codes as a means to prevent unionization and collective bargaining. If companies were really serious about ending abusive working conditions, they argue, then they would welcome international agreements to promote core labor standards and they would help workers to organize. On the other hand, the use of codes could be a way to create a "space" for organizing when the political regime in place is repressive (Shailor 1998). Critics of the union position against corporate codes suggest that labor in industrialized countries only wants to raise wages and improve working conditions abroad to reduce competition from cheap labor in a new form of protectionism.

One of the biggest points of difference between business and labor activists—besides unionization itself—is over the issue of wages. Many activists argue that workers in developing countries are simply not paid a fair wage. They insist that companies commit to paying a living wage instead of the legal minimum wage. The unions participating in the AIP withdrew largely over this issue. Most companies commit to paying the legal minimum wage, although in some countries, the government may deliberately set this low to attract foreign investment.[79]

Nevertheless, private sector initiatives could be one avenue for exporting labor standards from high-standard to low-standard countries without resorting to government mandate. These standards could establish a floor on global working conditions. Although it is hard to see at times, these initiatives are a breakthrough in relations between the private sector and society. Major companies are admitting publicly that they are responsible for the welfare of workers, at home and abroad. Even some unions and labor advocates take the position that voluntary self-regulation is a way to set minimum standards, raise consciousness about the need for standards, and provide guidance for national laws in the absence of a good governmental framework.

Businesses that adopt voluntary standards can enhance their reputation and improve product sales, employee recruitment, and productivity—all of which provide a needed competitive edge in world markets. Just as important, industry leaders view self-regulation as a potentially effective tool to prevent further government regulation. Indeed, most business leaders are firmly opposed to stronger international labor standards and especially oppose attempts to link trade and labor standards under the WTO. Participation in collective efforts to set standards and monitor them may help industries develop a positive relationship with industrialized country governments, although it is not as clear that it will improve relations with host governments abroad. There is even the possibility that these initiatives will improve relations with unions and labor and human rights advocates by reducing hostility and suspicion, although this is doubtful. At a minimum, the evolution of corporate codes has been toward more dialogue and partnership between corporate leaders and civil society organizations.

The systems of monitoring described above are still very much in their infancy. Mattel managers are very proud of their independent auditing system, and SAI has great hopes for SA 8000. Because they are still evolving, they are subject to much criticism. Despite this, if industry self-regulation is to have any effect at all, monitoring will be a critical element for everyone to assess progress from year to year. The information requirements for effective monitoring, however, are tremendous. One buyer might have agreements with literally thousands of suppliers, and each of those suppliers has their own suppliers. It is impossible for any one company to police that many facilities located around the world. This is why systems such as SA 8000 hold the greatest promise—each separate facility would seek out its own certification, and ultimately the hope is that buyers would only contract with certified factories.

Governments in industrialized countries may view private sector voluntary initiatives as a means to reduce public pressure to apply

sanctions and other punitive measures against low-standard countries. For governments in emerging markets, however, these initiatives pose a real challenge. From their point of view, foreign corporations, in league with activist organizations and unions and even their
home country governments, are interfering in local affairs. In fact,
some of what the companies propose is positively subversive. Representatives of developing countries can accuse the companies of creating inequities between workers in export industries and all others.
The codes that companies attempt to implement abroad are developed elsewhere, rarely with any local input. The price of entry into
world markets may be getting higher, which may reduce the comparative advantage of low-wage countries. Both the wto and oecd are
exploring whether cooperative agreements among businesses on
labor standards will distort trade flows, act as a nontariff barrier, and
perhaps even violate antitrust law.

4

The Case of Information Privacy

THE INFORMATION REVOLUTION has put a whole new set of issues on the international agenda. Throughout the 1980s and 1990s, governments around the world deregulated and privatized old-line industries such as telecommunications (Drake 1999). Computers transformed business practices and facilitated the expansion of TNCs and global business networks. The creation and commercialization of the Internet led to the development of entirely new industries, transformed older sectors of the economy, and provided entirely new services for citizens, governments, and businesses. Excitement over the opportunities created by this "new economy" has been tempered, however, by the challenge of creating an appropriate social and legal framework within which it can operate.

The central debate running through much of the discussion of the information economy has been over the degree to which public authorities need to reform old regulatory frameworks, create new ones, or simply leave the information industries alone. Laws forbidding pornography and hate speech have been undermined by the ease with which photos and words can be transferred across national borders. It is difficult, though not impossible, for national governments to limit the access of their citizens to online information. Traditional ideas about the protection of intellectual property rights have been overturned by the digitalization of everything from books to music to films, which allows the easy and nearly free replication and transfer of copyrighted works. Even property itself has been redefined, as recent battles over how to allocate Internet domain names demonstrate. One of the central areas in which commercial and social interests collide internationally is in the area of information privacy.

Privacy is the right of individuals to control the collection and use of personal information. It includes a wide range of issues, including everything from wiretapping to genetic identification systems to freedom of information. In online transactions, it covers the content of what is found online and offline, including censorship issues; spamming, or the unauthorized use of someone's e-mail address; and the personal information collected in commercial and government databases and then transferred, combined with information in other databases, and sold or exchanged with other entities. These databases can contain information such as travel profiles, cable television subscriptions, caller ID, online cookies, digital cash, and e-mail. The privacy of these databases and exchanges of information among them has become particularly important in interstate politics, as increasingly interconnected economies culturally collide over how to address public fears regarding how personal data are used or abused.

The decentralized, open, global character of one of the main transmission sources for personal data—the Internet—makes it difficult to design and implement effective regulations through top-down, government-by-government approaches. Industry representatives explicitly argue that they can regulate themselves effectively (eschewing any use of the words "social responsibility"). National regulatory authorities range from skeptical to fully supportive of this industry position, with little international consensus on the appropriate mechanisms and standards for international privacy protection.

The right to personal privacy is considered a basic legal right in most modern political systems, and worldwide, many societies recognize privacy as a fundamental human right (Banisar 2000). The degree to which any individual can expect personal information to be protected from others, including the government, is a defining feature of political and social systems. In an idealized past, people lived in communities in which everyone knew each other intimately, and privacy was limited by social custom. With the development of the modern state, large government bureaucracies became capable of systematically collecting personal data about masses of individuals. As government capacity grew, the danger that bureaucrats and politicians would abuse this capability led to fears of "big brother" monitoring everyone. Democratic societies have created legal systems to protect individuals from their own government's intrusions into their personal lives. Due to historical abuses of privacy by fascist and communist governments, European societies are particularly sensitive about this, and most have established strong privacy protections, treating privacy not just as a legal right but as a human right.

Today, many people perceive the main threat to privacy coming from the ability of large corporate bureaucracies to collect personal data on a grand scale. Recent technological advancements give business enterprises a previously unheard-of capacity to collect and use information about individuals in new ways. Every time someone provides a retailer or service provider with their name, address, and other identifying information, that information can be collected, organized, and even matched with information from other databases, to be recombined and used for purposes unknown to the original provider of personal data. Every time someone goes online and visits a web site, their every move can be tracked and identified. Any information or image placed on the World Wide Web can be viewed by millions of people anywhere in the world who have access to a networked computer. All of this personal information is contained in databases housed around the world and interconnected by the global telecommunications infrastructure. Corporations can use the network to process data in locations around the world, with records perhaps collected in Great Britain, entered in databases in the Philippines, and finally used in the United States—and individuals have little control over this transfer of data across national borders.

Business interests argue that the collection of personal data provides benefits to consumers and citizens. Merchants can provide consumers with a more personalized or customized transaction, responding instantly and often proactively to their tastes and interests. With the growth of the Internet, an ever-increasing number of transactions take place between the consumer and the retailer, with none of the traditional intermediaries. The benefits from collecting these data go not just to consumers, however, but to other businesses too. Each firm can transact business electronically directly with other firms, such as their suppliers and business partners, without regard to location or nationality.[80] Those business transactions often depend on the exchange of personal data about individual customers.

One of the central issues in the debate over information privacy is the ability of any individual to control the use and dissemination of *personally identifiable* information (that is, name, address, social security or identification number, and phone number). The expansion of electronic databases and data mining techniques threatens to connect such personal markers with more intimate information, creating a profile of one person's consumer habits, medical conditions, social activities, political and religious affiliations, and financial status. The data may be collected online as an individual uses the World Wide Web, or it may be collected offline any time a person fills out a form or application for a service. For online transactions, opinion polls indicate that privacy is the number one concern of users.[81]

There are a number of different kinds of perceived threats from the large-scale collection and transfer of personal data, falling into two categories: use and access. Many people are worried about what use will be made of personally identifiable data. For instance, medical information could be used by insurers to deny claims, or financial information could be used to deny loans. A related concern is that data freely given for one purpose may be used for another, such as when information collected by one firm is sold to another for marketing purposes, including the use of e-mail addresses for mass distribution of sales pitches. Databases may even be combined to match up the limited data contained in each one in order to develop a much more comprehensive picture of each person. Many critics decry the lack of control an individual has over the use of their own data, including the lack of recourse if the information is incorrect. A further, related concern is the question of who has access to the data and whether information collected and transmitted, especially across national lines, is secure from prying eyes. The security of databases, especially from government intrusion, is at the center of discussions about encryption policy (Bessette and Haufler 2001).

Individuals have certain core expectations regarding privacy issues. Most people expect autonomy, that is, if you do not affirmatively disclose information about yourself, then no one should be able to find out that information. Most have an expectation of control over what happens to their personal information once they give it out and prefer that information given remains confidential unless they give permission to share it. Privacy advocates argue that good policy, whether it is by the government or the private sector, should enable the consumer to know what the privacy policy of any entity is, to choose whether to give out personal information, to be given notice about what happens to personal data after it is given, and to know where to go to correct any misinformation or abuses.

The questions then become: Who is best placed to make those assurances, and how should it be done? Should governments institute strict and enforceable privacy policies? Can it be done through private sector self-regulation? What role will technology play in privacy debates? Public opinion has put great pressure on governments to intervene in this area. In response, the private sector has developed a variety of methods to protect personal privacy, largely in an attempt to prevent government intervention. The degree to which industry self-regulation provides adequate protections has become a divisive issue both within the United States—the largest information economy— and between the United States and its economic partners, particularly in Europe. The first section in this chapter discusses the background and development of industry self-regulation of privacy issues, within the context of a deep divide between the major information economies across the Atlantic. The next section analyzes how risk, reputation, and learning shape the policy outcomes resulting from the interaction of business, the public, and governments. The final section examines the issues of enforcement, certification, and accountability, which highlight the problems and promises of industry self-regulation in this issue area.

Industry Self-Regulation, Privacy Codes, and New Technology

The private sector is under extreme competitive pressures to increase productivity and gain competitive advantage by making the fullest possible use of the new information technologies. Industries from banking to manufacturing to online retailing all want to obtain information about consumers. They want to target them for marketing, to tailor products and services to their needs, and to weed out the individuals in whom they are not interested.[82] Many firms understand that consumers and business partners will not provide information or use new online technologies unless they have confidence in the medium. Despite the seeming explosion in the use of the Internet, e-commerce, and business-to-business transactions, many in business believe that we are only in the early stages in the development of this new market. One of the keys to expansion is to assure users of their privacy, or at least let them know when information is being collected and how it is being used.

Privacy is not a new issue, but it arises in new ways given the capabilities of computer and global telecommunications technologies. In 1973, the U.S. Department of Health, Education, and Welfare laid out a Code of Fair Information Practices for the U.S. government and its use of records on citizens. A similar code was adopted by IBM and then the Business Roundtable in the 1970s. The Code of Fair Information Practices provides the foundation for modern regulatory standards regarding information practices in both the public and private sectors. It recommends that organizations provide notice if they collect personal information; individuals must be able to find out what information is in a record; there must be some way to prevent the information from being used for anything other than the original purpose; there must be some way to correct or revise a record; and the organization that collects information must make sure it is accurate, secure, and not misused (Privacy Journal 2000). A large portion of the current privacy debate centers on how to apply these principles to online exchanges.

Starting in the 1970s, policy makers began to discuss the issue of privacy protection in data transfers. The Europeans began legislating on this issue long before the Internet became a commercial reality. Over a decade ago, they recognized the problems inherent in the new information technology:

> As the volume of transborder flows increases, the control possibilities diminish. It becomes much more difficult, for example, to identify the countries through which data will transit before reaching the authorized recipient. Problems of data security and confidentiality are heightened when data are piped through communication lines which traverse countries where little or no attention is accorded to issues of data protection . . . When advanced communications networks enable businessmen on foreign travels to access their enterprises' data bases via hand-held computers plugged into sockets available in airports and to

down-load data instantaneously into their computers across vast distances, the issue of national regulation of transborder data flows becomes problematic indeed. (Council of Europe 1989, 14)

The first, and for many years the only, multilateral standard for transnational exchange of data was the voluntary OECD Guidelines on the Protection of Privacy and Transborder Flows of Personal Data, adopted in 1980. These guidelines set specific standards for how nations should treat individually identifiable information collected in commercial databases. These are simply guidelines for countries seeking to develop a national framework to handle new privacy concerns. They had little direct influence and were soon overtaken by advancing technology.

The U.S. government under the Clinton administration deliberately chose not to regulate in this new economic area. This is partly due to an ideological reluctance to interfere with the new economy—the source of the longest economic boom in recorded U.S. history. It is also partly due to the institutional structure of the U.S. political system and the existing patchwork system of privacy protection. The U.S. legal system does not address privacy issues in a comprehensive manner.[83] Traditionally, multiple agencies and levels of government have handled privacy law, each taking a small piece of the overall policy domain. As a privacy concern gains public attention in a particular industry sector, say in the banking or medical industries, the government may propose new legislation and regulation to address narrow concerns.[84] Particular privacy problems may generate their own special attention, as with the demand to protect children's online privacy. The system is fragmented across different government agencies and levels of government—federal, state, and local.[85]

Strong privacy protections exist for the public sector to ensure that government bureaucrats handle personal information appropriately. For instance, the Internal Revenue Service is governed by strict rules and punishments that apply to anyone with access to tax information. In the United States there was up until recently little oversight of the private sector and the privacy issues raised by commercial exchange of personal data. Privacy issues inherent in the international transfer of data are not addressed at all.

In a few commercial sectors, industry in both the United States and elsewhere has long taken a lead in developing strong standards for protecting personal data. Business leaders in banking, for instance, know well that its customers expect and even demand utter confidentiality about their financial transactions (particularly Swiss banks), which are now contained in digital format in databases that are interconnected, both nationally and internationally. In fact, the financial sector is one of the most prominent users of encryption technology that assures the security of its data transfers. Recent changes in the industry due to deregulation and mergers across financial sectors raise new privacy concerns. Critics charge the financial sector with lax oversight of how personal information gets transferred from one business to another within a single financial institution. For instance, some people object to the fact that when they fill out a mortgage application that data may be given to an insurance subsidiary or sold to a third party.

The lack of a comprehensive system of privacy protection in the United States and the Clinton administration's commitment to self-regulation by the information industries has come squarely up against the brick wall of EU law. European political systems tend to have strong centralized government protections of personal data of all sorts. They may be behind the United States in Internet usage and e-commerce, but they have been proactive in addressing the privacy problems they foresaw. Many individual countries have developed national privacy policies, but the European Commission has been a strong promoter of regional regulation of this issue.

The Europeans clearly have gone down a different path than the United States. Public concern about and awareness of information privacy issues are much higher in Europe than in the United States. European governments have sought to establish a legal framework of privacy protections in advance of the full development and widespread use of modern information technologies. For instance, France established its Commission Nationale de l'Informatique et des Libertés (CNIL) to deal with information issues as early as 1978. Each country in the EU has established (or plans to establish) a data protection agency, such as the CNIL in France and the Data Protection Registrar in the United Kingdom. Those who collect information—both commercially and noncommercially—must register with the authority and describe their data protection policies.

The United States and the EU have been negotiating for the last decade over the issue of data collection and data transfer across national borders. The two sides unfortunately have settled on two diametrically opposed approaches for resolving privacy issues. The European perspective favors a top-down, comprehensive government regulatory approach, including harmonization of competing national and regional regimes. The U.S. perspective favors a more decentralized approach that involves selective national regulation of specific subissues, leaving the rest to private sector self-regulation—or to no regulation at all.

In the early 1980s the EU passed a fairly comprehensive set of regulations for transborder data flows. The 1981 Convention for the Protection of Individuals with Regard to Automatic Processing of Personal Data was passed by the Council of Europe in 1981, at the very beginning of the information revolution. The goal at both the national and regional levels was to approach all privacy issues in a centralized and enforceable manner. The convention stipulates that a member state can treat transborder data flows of personal information differently from other commercial exchanges if they have laws about the treatment of personal data and automated databases, except when the other country has "equivalent protection." Such data can also be treated differently if they will transit through a contracting party on its way to a noncontracting party simply to avoid the legislation (Council of Europe 1981). Commercial data collectors are required to use the data only for the purposes originally specified; they are not allowed to process data revealing such personal characteristics as race, religion, or medical conditions except under domestic legal guarantees; data cannot be given or sold to others unless required by domestic law; and all information must be corrected, updated, or deleted as required by law. Over the course of the next decade, however, only twelve members states ratified the convention.[86]

By the late 1980s, as the new global information-based economy gained ground, the differences between the European and U.S. approaches to the privacy concerns raised by massive data collection began to create potential new problems. More and more corporations were implementing new information systems using the latest technology. They operated their data collection and analysis through transnational systems that transferred personal data back and forth across the

Atlantic Ocean. The use of the Internet—as a global medium to buy and sell and, more importantly, to collect consumer information—began to skyrocket. The news media began to scrutinize the privacy protection policies of commercial data collectors, and the public became more aware of the ways in which their personally identifiable information could be collected, combined, transferred, and sold.

Horror stories of identity theft, fraud, and misuse of medical information began to stimulate public concern and action by the mid-1990s. In the United States, the Electronic Privacy Information Center (EPIC) began to lobby the U.S. government, persistently arguing in support of stronger regulation. The nonprofit Center for Democracy and Technology directed its efforts at both the public and private sectors and urged more effective self-regulation by industry. The American Civil Liberties Union (ACLU), the Electronic Frontier Foundation, and others mobilized primarily around freedom of speech issues. The London-based Privacy International, founded in 1990 as a human rights watchdog group with representatives in a dozen countries, focuses on government and corporate surveillance. Traditional consumer groups such as the Consumers Union have become active on this issue, informing and educating their members and the public about emerging privacy concerns. Numerous other groups have sprung up to advocate vastly different positions—from promotion of greater, more comprehensive, international regulation to a purely libertarian stance that consumers should be given property rights in their personal information and allowed to sell it.[87]

In response to increasing public attention, in part mobilized by these advocacy groups, the European Commission developed a new, even more comprehensive Data Protection Directive. It was put forward in 1995, to be implemented by the European Economic Area by October 1998, although few countries met this deadline. So far, the EU Data Protection Directive only applies automatically in the EU to the collection and transfer of information by public sector agencies but must be formally implemented by member governments to cover commercial firms. This newly revised data directive highlighted the divide between the United States and EU and became a huge source of tension in transatlantic relations during the mid-1990s.

The main source of transatlantic dissension became the implementation of principles under the data directive concerning the transfer of data outside the European Economic Area.[88] Under the provisions of Article 25 of the directive, no personal data can be transferred to third countries unless that country provides an adequate level of protection for the particular data transfer operation in question. The definition of "adequate" is vague, stating that this shall be assessed "in light of all the circumstances." These circumstances include the nature of the personal data, the country of origin and destination of the data, the purposes and duration of the data processing, the laws and international obligations of the destination country, relevant codes of conduct or rules, and any security measures taken with regard to that country (UK Data Protection Registrar 1999, 4–5). Ultimately, whoever is proposing to transfer data has to make a judgment on this matter. If they guess wrong, they may be subject to enforcement measures or to litigation. Even before any agreement was reached regarding the United States, Privacy International announced plans to track Europe's 200 largest data exporters and threatened litigation over transfers to the United States, believing that U.S. data protection does not meet the adequacy standards (IBM 1998).

The Clinton administration wanted to come to some consensus with the Europeans to establish an international regime for privacy protection. This new regime, however, was to be based primarily on industry self-regulation, the preferred U.S. approach. At a minimum, it would reconcile EU and U.S. approaches, without subjecting U.S. firms to EU strictures. Negotiations between the two sides clearly had the potential to lay the global ground rules for data privacy in the electronic age; however, the United States quickly found itself on a collision course with the EU. Prior to adopting the data directive in 1995, EU and U.S. representatives met repeatedly, but each side simply pushed their own preferred system.

Over the next few years, in repeated meetings, the United States steadfastly argued that personal information transferred to the United States would be adequately protected by industry self-regulation. The EU consistently refused to accept the U.S. system as adequate under the provisions of the data directive. The U.S. negotiators went back to the drawing board a number of times to modify their proposals while still clinging to self-regulation as the underlying principle for protecting privacy. Industry experts submitted reports and testimony to support the U.S. government position, but to no avail.

During this time, a variety of industry players began to develop an increasing number of self-regulatory policies and technologies to meet public expectations. They were also clearly responding to the threat of government intervention, both domestic and international. Moreover, industry professionals viewed themselves as highly competent to address the complex, emerging issues posed by the new information economy—more so than government bureaucrats (Spar and Busgang 1996). Industry producers and users had independently designed rules to govern many of the early aspects of computer, software, and Internet development, and they looked forward to continuing in this vein.[89] They believed then and still do that the success of new information technologies is due precisely to the lack of interference by government, and that government regulators simply do not have the capability to deal with the rapid changes and complex issues of the new information economy.[90]

American companies have taken the lead in launching voluntary efforts to protect privacy. A number of industry groups have sought to develop and promote self-regulatory efforts, such as the Online Privacy Alliance (OPA), the Internet Privacy Working Group, the Information Technology Industry Council, and the Internet Alliance.[91] Despite the appearance of consensus on these issues, however, the information industries are so competitive and the players change so rapidly because of mergers, acquisitions, alliances, and new entrants that it is difficult for them to work together consistently.[92] Despite this, as one industry report stated, "Political, technological, and economic trends are all driving companies to the high end, not the low end, of privacy protection" (Blackmer and Charyton 1998, 5).

A number of types of industry self-regulatory mechanisms have emerged in the past few years: standard setting, corporate codes, auditing and certification, and technological fixes. Individual companies, particularly web-based ventures, have promised to develop and publish corporate codes laying out a privacy policy that details standards to which they adhere. Internet service providers and online content providers, medical and financial industries, and advertisers all have developed industrywide codes of conduct that typically include standards for protection of individual privacy. Traditional industries not always associated with the high-technology world but increasingly dependent on international transmission of data have been at the forefront of developing standards for information privacy. For example, the American Bankers Association, which already had strict confidentiality provisions, developed a new privacy code for its members to deal with changes in information technology in the past decade. Most of these codes or privacy policies contain a commitment to provide notice and disclosure of information collection, to detail what is done with the information, to promise security of information, and to provide choice and consent. One of the key debates between privacy advocates and industry concerns "opt-in" versus "opt-out" provisions. Advocates prefer to have a system in which individuals have to volunteer their personal data; industry tends to prefer a system in which merchants or service providers collect information but the user can volunteer to opt-out of this data collection.

The most prominent initiative is TRUSTe, a nonprofit organization established by the Electronic Frontier Foundation and Commercenet in 1996 that has become the dominant force in privacy certification. Its motto is "Building a web you can believe in." Members of TRUSTe can place a certification symbol or "watermark" on their web sites as a third-party assurance of compliance with a set of privacy standards.[93] This voluntary initiative includes an auditing system to ensure that web site owners uphold their privacy commitments, and the program also responds to consumer complaints with a dispute resolution process. TRUSTe launched a test run in 1996 with 100 companies, and today more than 800 web sites sport the TRUSTe seal, including all the portal sites, over half the top 100 sites, and two-thirds of the twenty most-frequented sites (Steer 1999). In response to the EU Data Directive and Safe Harbor agreement (described below), TRUSTe now has a Safe Harbor Seal program, which assists companies to self-certify to the Department of Commerce under Safe Harbor provisions. TRUSTe also has a special Children's Program, addressing one of the more popular issues in the privacy debate. TRUSTe 's Privacy Partnership Program also seeks to educate the public about privacy issues and advocates with web site owners to increase commitment to privacy protections.

The other leading privacy program is by the U.S. Better Business Bureau, which has long been the main recourse for consumer complaints of all sorts in the United States. It recently launched BBBonline. The BBBonline program establishes six standards that companies with the BBBonline Seal must follow. Like TRUSTe, BBBonline has a motto too: "Say what you do, do what you say, and have it verified" (BBBOnline 2000). It has two programs—the Reliability Seal Program, to assure consumers that they are dealing with a trusted online merchant; and the Privacy Seal Program, to assure compliance with privacy standards. BBBOnline is international, processing applications from over twenty countries and certifying international corporations. Over 9,000 sites are certified with the Reliability Seal, but only 723 participate in the Privacy Seal, indicating that this privacy program has yet to take off (BBBOnline 2000).

The accounting industry also has woken up to the fact that it can play a role in an entirely new market for privacy assurances. The American Institute of Certified Public Accountants (AICPA) developed the WebTrust program, a set of privacy practices for commercial web sites that includes labeling and a training program for certified public accountants. It does not, however, include a system of recourse for individuals, or accountability for errors and misuse. Both TRUSTe and AICPA are working with Verisign, a technology company, to develop a digital identification that will allow consumers to know whether a merchant is really certified, or if it is using a seal without authorization. Consumers and business users, it is assumed, will choose to transact business and share information with certified companies, and this, in turn, will drive the demand for more privacy protection. These labeling and certification programs have only existed for a few years. Most major corporations have adopted some form of posted privacy policy, and hundreds now have the TRUSTe or BBBOnline Seal.

Another main avenue for industry self-regulation is through technological fixes, often hand-in-hand with new corporate codes. These include encryption software (to allow users to make their electronic transactions secure) and anonymizers (to allow use of online services without revealing any personal information). Many technology firms are feverishly working to develop the software that would allow consumers to choose how they want their information to be handled. Other companies seek to develop software to assist companies trying to meet consumer privacy concerns. For example, NCR, a major data warehouse group, recently unveiled software that they said would assist financial institutions, retailers, and others who store consumer information to meet or exceed requirements for privacy in the United States and EU. The most significant initiative, and the one with the most potential (though also the most technically complex), is the Platform for Privacy Preferences (P3P), a joint effort of the World Wide Web Consortium. P3P is a set of standards that will enable web sites to show their privacy practices easily, in a standardized and automatic manner. It is supposed to allow individuals and even entire nations to choose the collection, use, and disclosure standards appropriate for them.[94] P3P is supposed to be a partial solution to privacy concerns that preserves choice in part by providing full notice of privacy options. Members of this consortium include many of the biggest names, such as IBM, Microsoft, and AOL. Nonindustry groups, such as the Center for Democracy and Technology, have also provided input into the design of P3P. These standards are not yet fully implemented, although Microsoft has said it will include P3P in its next version of Internet Explorer.

Esther Dyson, a supporter of TRUSTe and a key promoter of the information revolution, argues that individual choice must be the key to any privacy program. She believes that privacy disclosure policies can be effective, if consumers would just "get off their butts and demand it." She argues that insurers and investors need to be more active in auditing company practices (Welte 2000). But many consumers would prefer complete privacy, not a disclosure policy, allowing no access at all to their personal data. If enough of them choose *en masse* to refuse to give out information, it could stop cold many of the new commercial practices that rely on collecting personal data. Many people, contrary to what Dyson and others would prefer, simply would rather have the government set and enforce privacy regulations.

These self-regulatory systems should, in theory, be self-enforcing, because merchants have such a strong economic incentive to attract consumers and business partners by establishing a positive reputation— by being trustworthy. Customer information is being viewed increasingly as "nonmonetary currency," and the way to obtain the data often requires building in a level of trust with users. Many consumers today fear the Internet and e-commerce transactions because of privacy concerns.[95] In fact, loss of personal privacy is a top concern of Americans today (Horovitz 2001). Internet users generally would be more likely to purchase online if they knew the online merchant had a privacy policy, and privacy and security are the number one barriers to online buying, according to a recent survey (TRUSTe 2000a). An increasing number of firms realize that if they cannot convince the public that their self-regulatory initiatives are working, then they may either lose a substantial amount of business or face government action. Microsoft and IBM recently announced they would not advertise on any web site that did not have an adequate privacy protection policy, thus enforcing their privacy standards on those with whom they do business.

All of this industry action occurred while the United States and EU were trying to negotiate their differences over the application of the EU Data Directive. When the directive came into force in 1998, the EU threatened to cut off all data transfers between Europe and the United States. This threat propelled representatives of both sides into even more intensive negotiations, while the European Commission temporarily delayed implementation of this provision. The U.S. administration proposed in November 1998 that a "safe harbor" be created for U.S.-based corporations that individually met European demands, arguing that these firms should be allowed to receive data from Europe. The exact details of this safe harbor were—and still are—very controversial. Early proposals included providing a safe harbor to companies that joined a private sector privacy program, which would be a form of self-regulation not entirely trusted by everyone. The United States then reworked its original proposals to try to meet objections from the EU. Key aspects of the plan have to do with notification of individuals about what information is being collected and for what purpose, and choice over what will be done with the data once collected.

The industry group OPA, in its white paper of November 1998, argued that the "collective effect of 'layered' regulatory and self-regulatory measures creates 'adequate' safeguards for the protection of personal information collected online in the United States" (Blackmer and Charyton 1998, 1).[96] The OPA argues that self-regulatory programs, such as publicly announced policies and codes of conduct including those of the OPA itself, would be backed up by the enforcement power of domestic institutions such as the Federal Trade Commission and state and local agencies. Specific sectoral issues would be protected by law. In either case, consumers would be able to bring litigation to settle claims that a member had violated the OPA standards (Blackmer and Charyton 1998, 2). Despite the positive tone of this report, it was clear that most firms were dragging their feet, refusing to adopt any self-regulatory policy, free riding on the OPA's efforts, and hoping that the government would never step in and put limits on the dynamic information sector of the economy.

In 1999, in the Framework for Global Electronic Commerce, the Clinton administration laid out what it saw as the key elements of effective self-regulation: substantive rules, the means to ensure consumers know those rules and whether companies comply with them, and the ability of consumers to have some recourse in the case of violations (U.S. White House 1999).[97] Policy makers, particularly Vice President Gore and Special White House Advisor Ira Magaziner, explicitly stated their preference for industry self-regulation instead of government intervention, with legislation and regulation only in cases in which there is evidence of harm, such as children's privacy.

The European Commission Working Party (Directorate General xv) weighed in with at most a lukewarm endorsement of the safe harbor proposals. Its preliminary opinion in February 1999 stated that "the patchwork of narrowly focused sectoral laws and self-regulatory rules presently existent in the United States cannot be relied upon to provide adequate protection in all cases for personal data transferred from the European Union" (European Commission Data Protection Working Party 1999, 1). The OECD Guidelines of 1980 had to be minimum standards for transfer of data to third parties outside the European Economic Area, and outside the safe harbor scheme.

Consumer groups also reacted critically to the safe harbor proposal. The Trans-Atlantic Consumer Dialogue (TACD) argued that the proposal lacked an effective means of enforcement or redress for privacy violations. It also, according to TACD, placed unreasonable burdens on consumers and forced Europeans to give up some of their existing rights. At a meeting in April 1999, the TACD urged the European Commission and the Ministers of the European Council to reject the safe harbor proposal and recommended negotiation of an international convention on privacy protection (TACD 1999).

Finally, in July 2000, the European Commission approved the Safe Harbor Agreement, despite objections from the European Parliament and many privacy groups. The United States and the EU finally agreed on an information privacy regime that would be a compromise between European and American positions. U.S. companies that collect personal information about people in Europe would need to adhere to EU privacy protection rules, especially when they transfer that information back to the United States. The agreement applies mainly to U.S. banks, airlines, and MNCs. Online data collection would be exempt, at least for now. Companies wanting to do business in Europe would register with the U.S. Commerce Department to declare their intention to abide by EU rules and would be subject to legal action in the United States and enforcement by the Federal Trade Commission if they failed. Approximately forty companies have signed on to it so far. This outcome in many ways reflects the preferences of industry in the United States, allowing for continued self-regulation and the "layered" approach favored by the OPA. Within months of the agreement, Privacy International asked the British Data Protection Commissioner to investigate Amazon.com for improper transfer of personal information. The U.S. Congress also may hold hearings to reevaluate whether American companies should be subject to European privacy law in this way.

Risk, Reputation, and Learning

Clearly, one of the main forces driving the industries to self-regulate is the threat of government regulation. In Europe, the regulatory system was largely in place although not fully developed or updated to take account of the changing nature of the information revolution. In the United States, the Clinton administration strongly supported industry self-regulation, promoting it widely, but without complete success in terms of public opinion. Congress and state legislatures were considering legislation covering selective pieces of the privacy issue, such as medical information. In December 2000, the Clinton administration put forth new regulations at the federal level on the privacy of medical records. That same month Congress passed the Children's Internet Protection Act requiring schools receiving federal funds for Internet access to install filtering and blocking software. The mixed messages being sent in the U.S. context were overwhelmed by the imminent imposition of regulations from Europe. There, in many ways, a different debate was taking place. Most governments, and the EU, accepted a strong role for action by public authorities on privacy issues. The focus often was on personal information collected by governments, and not by commercial organizations.[98] Much of industry action was directed at providing a reason for governments not to regulate.

The intense competitiveness of industry today, particularly the information sector, makes it difficult for any one company to shut off the flow of personal data or to refuse to take advantage of new information collection technologies. As privacy fears balloon, as they have in recent years, it will also be difficult for those who take advantage of these technologies to avoid adopting some form of privacy policy. Advocates of TRUSTe, for instance, believe that today "privacy seal programs are utilized by enough highly visible sites so that displaying a recognized privacy seal—and thus living up to the standards upheld by the privacy seal program—becomes a necessary tool in a competitive environment" (Steer 1999,1). One survey in January 1999 revealed that, of 361 web sites visited, 92.8 percent collected some personal information, and 65.9 percent had some type of privacy disclosure (Georgetown University 1999). Another survey of the top 100 sites visited by consumers reported that 98 percent collected personal data of some sort, and 93 percent posted a privacy disclosure of some sort (OPA 1999). Collective efforts to self-regulate make much more sense than individual initiatives, but so far the field is dominated by only a handful of them. Individual firms, and a few key industry associations, have been leaders in this area. But the design of some of these initiatives, especially those that do not allow for recourse, clearly favors the private sector. The test for privacy seal programs will come not just with widespread adoption, but with successes in monitoring, enforcement, and dispute settlement.

Many observers have commented that e-commerce would expand if consumers and businesses had confidence in the medium and if they trusted the partners with whom they work. In other words, reputation matters. The web sites most used by consumers tend to be the big names, such as Amazon.com, or the online counterparts of trusted retailers. Individual companies such as IBM advocate strong privacy policies in part to reinforce an already well-developed reputation for integrity. TRUSTe explicitly makes the link between consumer trust and brand name: "Gaining the trust of your customers is perhaps the most critical ingredient in establishing your brand. Research shows time and again that users have an overriding desire to control the uses of their personal information" (TRUSTe 2000a). However, there are many online and offline major data collectors that are relatively anonymous. Only a few companies have acquired a bad reputation for abusing personal privacy, such as Doubleclick, which tracks where people go and what they do on the World Wide Web.

Two different kinds of learning are significant in this case. First, the public itself has had to be educated about privacy problems in an information age. Generally, the public has not been mobilized on this issue, despite the media horror stories that have created fear about online and offline theft of information or identity. Some nonprofit groups, including industry-based ones such as TRUSTe, have launched educational campaigns. These educational efforts have also been targeted at businesses, particularly web site operators, to convince them that they should adopt privacy codes as part of good business practices.

A good deal of the learning going on in this case has been of the political sort too. Industries that thought they were immune to politics and outside of normal regulatory frameworks found themselves at the center of very real political debates with significant consequences for how they did business. They discovered that government still has authority, even in the new economy. Despite globalization, industry leaders discovered that political preferences vary profoundly across nations, and that this variation can produce deep divides between countries, with the potential to cripple a sector that sees itself as global.

Enforcement, Certification, and Accountability

The privacy policies adopted by many firms are simply statements of policy, without any real enforcement provisions. Collective initiatives such as TRUSTe and BBBOnline rely on certification as a tool to obtain compliance. Those certified are monitored, and those accused of violations must participate in an alternative dispute resolution program. Violators can be investigated, audited, have their seal revoked, terminated from the program, sued for breach of contract, and even referred to federal authorities. So far, the limits of this system are only beginning to be tested. Privately developed standards can be enforced in national courts or administrative hearings, and some privacy advocates are exploring this. Privacy International has threatened to bring legal action against U.S.-based companies for violating British or EU privacy law.

The Safe Harbor Agreement between the United States and EU is an unusual mix of public and private authority. It preserves the preference for government action that we see in Europe, while also preserving the industry self-regulation currently in favor in Washington. U.S. companies can maintain that they are not regulated, yet they promise to abide by the provisions of EU law. If they do not comply with those provisions, they can suffer the very real punishment of a cut-off of data transfers from Europe.

The technological solutions for privacy issues, such as encryption or other software, attempt to sidestep the issues of accountability and enforcement. They focus on the individual who provides information, instead of primarily on what the information collector can or cannot do. The new technologies are supposed to make it possible for individuals to make their own choices. Even if the technologies are made available, however, it is not clear that many individuals or firms will rush to adopt them. Most companies appear to be taking a wait and see attitude, only taking action on privacy concerns when the threat of government action becomes real.

Early surveys of web sites show that only a small percentage display a privacy policy for viewers. This has been held up as a sign that self-regulation does not work. More recent surveys, however, show that more and more web sites are at least posting privacy policies, although it is not clear what their content is or whether it is anything beyond a promise to protect personal data. Many online services collect data without individual consumers even knowing it is happening; for instance, software can monitor the "clickstream" of the user as he or she visits different web sites. The technological solutions proposed by different groups have yet to be implemented fully. TRUSTe, although invested with high hopes by many, had a poor start, with relatively little support from industry. Recently, more web sites have begun using the TRUSTe system, and the Internet Content Coalition, an alliance of content providers, recently endorsed it. The WebTrust program has only certified a handful of web sites so far.

These self-regulatory systems have begun to be tested by recent cases. For instance, RealNetworks, which is certified by TRUSTe, apparently collected globally unique identifiers from users of their products, which violated the privacy of those individuals unknowingly transmitting this information. It appeared to be a real breakdown in the privacy certification program. The TRUSTe privacy seal is for the Real-Networks web site, but not for its software products, which are located on personal computers. TRUSTe and RealNetworks both agreed this was a problem that could undermine the trust consumers have in Real-Networks and in the TRUSTe program itself. The outcry from this incident gave industry self-regulation a black eye. Afterwards, both TRUSTe and RealNetworks agreed to develop a program that addresses privacy issues built into software. The program they devised includes third-party auditing of RealNetworks privacy policies, more notice about data collection, appointment of a RealNetworks privacy officer, and other actions. All of this points to the rapidity with which technological change can overturn newly established policies. In this case, the managers of the TRUSTe program designed it for data collection that occurs via web sites and did not at first realize the significance of new kinds of software that reside on a person's computer and transmit data back to the web site of the software developer (TRUSTe 2000b).

One of the biggest issues remaining, however, is that of accountability or recourse. Few privacy policies include an easily used process to contest misuse or mistakes in collecting data. The systems of recourse embodied in self-regulatory initiatives such as TRUSTe have not been tested. Many consumers do not know their rights, or who to go to in order to protect them. Under the safe harbor provisions negotiated between United States and EU, the self-regulation of corporations will be backed by the enforcement powers of government. This too has yet to be tested. It is still too early to tell whether the current system will be effective.

THIS CHAPTER FOCUSED PRIMARILY on the United States and Europe for several reasons. They have made the most advances in moving toward an information economy. They are also the most deeply involved in wrestling with the issue of information privacy. Finally, they are the home countries for the majority of the global information industry, which is the source for these new variations on old debates over privacy rights. Both regulatory and self-regulatory developments in the United States and EU have the potential to be the basis for global rules in this area.

What is striking in this case are the profound differences between European and American attitudes toward the role of government in protecting privacy. The Europeans are deeply suspicious of industry self-regulation on something that touches what they view as a basic human right and prefer to have those rights protected in law and backed by governmental authority. Paradoxically, their greatest fears when it comes to privacy are that the government itself will abuse its access to personal data. The American public, while also suspicious of industry, is even more leery of government intervention, especially in an area so vital to the modern economy as the information sector. The cultural predispositions of these two led each down totally different paths—but paths that intersected because of the inherently global nature of modern telecommunications and information exchanges.

The new technologies are reaching into more corners of the world each year. Global business is rapidly taking advantage of the possibilities for connecting far-flung operations via telecommunications and computer technology. Information exchanges increasingly occur not just among the most "wired" countries, but also with some of the least wired countries. Data entry, for instance, is often handled by workers in developing countries. The confidentiality of data may be compromised in countries not covered by any existing regulation or international agreements. The cultural differences in these developing countries with regard to the concept of privacy rights will be even more profound than the ones that bedeviled U.S. and EU negotiators. Technologies that allow entire countries to establish their own standards, either by implementing software on local servers or through labeling schemes that point consumers to merchants adhering to national standards, may preserve some ability of countries to determine their own levels of privacy protection. Or they may become weapons in the hands of repressive regimes.

Both the governmental and self-regulatory models are in a period of evolution and testing. Critics argue that the governmental model of top-down regulation may stifle innovation, limit the expansion of the information industries, and increase costs for a highly competitive industry. Supporters of the governmental model argue that it is the only way to protect privacy rights thoroughly and effectively, and this protection, in turn, will reassure individuals and businesses and encourage them to exploit fully the new media, leading to an expansion in the use of information technology. As the EU Data Directive is fully implemented across Europe, we will gain more evidence and insight into these two divergent positions. Critics of a voluntary system based on industry preferences argue that the industry has a stake in collecting data and therefore will not fully adhere to voluntary programs, which could undermine confidence in the system and limit the expansion of information exchanges. Supporters, however, argue that self-regulation and technological developments combined, in contrast to governmental mandates alone, may create a more effective, flexible, and usable system that is able to adjust quickly to rapid technological changes. This may be true, but business executives did not take the lead in educating the public about the ways in which new commercial practices compromised the individual's control over personal data. This raises public concern about how much we know about what information is collected and how it is used. Despite this, the increasing adoption and use of privacy seals and alternative dispute resolution mechanisms seem to indicate that the business community understands that public concern is real, that public concern has direct effects on markets, and that ultimately the public will push government to take action if business is unresponsive.

5

The Evolution of New Global Rules

THIS BOOK HAS SOUGHT to explore the issues raised when the private sector takes on a public role, specifically industry's trend toward self-regulation. It has examined how self-regulation plays out in three areas of global concern: environment, labor, and information privacy. This concluding chapter starts by comparing and contrasting these three cases of self-regulation. It examines the differences and similarities in the importance of risk, reputation, and learning in each case and offers an assessment of self-regulation in light of arguments about corporate power and the perception that this activity is simply a public relations policy. The next section analyzes the challenge that such corporate action makes to governments and discusses the alternative policies that governments can pursue. Industry self-regulation, to the degree it becomes common, also poses challenges to the business community itself and to society as a whole. The final section, therefore, provides a broader view of the results of industry self-regulation and speculates about what this means for governance in general.

The Cases: Environment, Labor, and Information

These three widely diverging cases illustrate some of the common factors pushing business leaders to adopt self-regulatory programs. At the same time, they demonstrate the deep differences in the weight accorded to these factors in the different issue areas. All of them clearly are driven by two overwhelming forces: the risk that governments will intervene, either nationally or internationally, to enforce rules on industry; and the risk that activists will mobilize locally and transnationally, organizing a campaign among consumers, investors, and shareholders and putting pressure on governments to take action against the companies. Three other factors played important roles in shaping how political risks led company leaders to turn to industry self-regulation: reputation, economic competition, and learning.

All three cases demonstrate how important the threat of national or international regulation was to the decision by corporate leaders to choose a self-regulatory strategy. In the environmental arena, new international rules have become increasingly common, covering everything from ozone depletion to biodiversity. There is increasing pressure to tie trade agreements to new environmental and labor standards, as NAFTA and the continuing debates on this regarding the WTO clearly show. The imminent imposition of European privacy rules on U.S.-based information companies mobilized the business community in a very direct way. At the national level, the threat of government regulation is greatest in the already highly regulated industrialized economies—not in the developing world where many of these problems exist. But political leaders in Europe and North America are clearly looking for ways to act against violations in developing countries, especially in the case of labor standards. The information privacy case, however, shows that the transnational use of self-regulation is not always primarily a North-South issue but can find a place in transactions among developed countries.

The business community appears to have widely differing perspectives on the advantages and disadvantages of a world with multiple, competing systems of law and regulation. An MNC able to conduct its business in countries with varying standards can use those differences as a source of competitive advantage and therefore would prefer either no regulation or voluntary self-regulation. Certainly, in labor-intensive industries, the existence of countries with varying levels of development and varying costs of labor can be a critical benefit. But differences among national systems can also be costly, especially for more complex industries. Companies that have to comply with myriad environmental standards and rules have argued that they do not care whether standards are set high or low, just so long as they are consistent across countries. They may prefer international harmonization of the rules of the game. However, even those executives who look favorably on the idea of establishing broad international standards hesitate to promote them for fear the negotiating process among states would produce multilateral rules that are unworkable, complex, hard to interpret, and anticompetitive. Corporate leaders prefer to deal with national governments on an individual basis because they are more confident of their ability to influence domestic politics.[99] In many cases, they may encourage domestic government regulation as a way to promote their economic advantage by limiting competition and innovation and by protecting markets.

The vaunted homogenization that is supposed to result from increased globalization has not wiped out the distinctive character of societies. When it comes to debates over regulation, sociocultural contexts still have a great deal of influence over how they play out. What is relevant in this context is the way in which the historical development of relations between business and government has influenced the debate over regulation and self-regulation even today. For instance, the United States and Europe have very different histories with regard to business–government relations. When it comes to the environment, corporations in the United States worry primarily about liability and therefore focus on compliance with national law and regulation. For years business interests have struggled against the Environmental Protection Agency, although now leaders in both business and government are looking for new ways to protect the environment while leaving room for flexibility in corporate decision making. Labor–management relations have always been very different in Europe compared to the United States. Unionization rates are higher in Europe, labor has much more political influence, and in the case of Germany, labor representatives sit on the boards of companies. In the United States, information technology firms are begging to be left alone, arguing that this brand-new economic arena should not be put in a government straitjacket. In contrast, European corporate interests tend to be more concerned with lobbying to influence the shape of national and EU regulations than they are in avoiding them altogether.

The growing power of transnational activist groups is the other main factor propelling business to adopt self-regulatory tactics. Every case, every issue, highlights the role of activism in changing the cost-benefit calculations of a firm. By targeting the reputation of a company and by pursuing strategies that affect a company's ability to operate, activist groups make it difficult for corporations to conduct business as usual. They use a wide variety of tactics, including everything from boycotts to lawsuits to—in extreme cases—sabotage. They are becoming quite adept at using the Internet to launch creative campaigns. For instance, the Rainforest Action Network organizes letter-writing campaigns from its web site against forest product and financial services companies. Even small groups can amplify their voice and reach across national boundaries. As the author of a recent report said, "Despite the fact that the business community has greater financial resources than these groups, corporations don't have the upper hand when it comes to Internet advocacy" (Pinkham 2000).[100] Environmental groups have been particularly effective at using the U.S. legal system against polluters abroad, and labor advocates are doing the same regarding sweatshop conditions in developing countries.

This kind of activism was strongest in the environmental and labor rights cases, with only weak—though significant—activism in the information privacy case. The latter may be changing, because many people consider privacy to be "the" issue of the information age. If activism on privacy increases, particularly in the countries where most information transactions are based, then more companies probably will strengthen their voluntary programs.

The same transnational activism that can threaten MNCs can also be mobilized to support working alongside them. Advocacy groups tend to push for industry self-regulation in areas where governments cannot or will not act. Therefore, they may seek out partnerships with corporations or industry groups, and assist in the design of corporate codes and voluntary programs. Such business–NGO partnerships are particularly common for labor and environmental issues (Murphy and Bendell 1997). Nevertheless, even as these groups work in partnership with the private sector in some areas, they are not shy about expressing their critical views of the same companies' actions in another. Greenpeace may work with business partners on an issue such as climate change while criticizing these same companies for not doing more. The Rainforest Action Network (RAN) may campaign against a forest products company, even if that company is a member—alongside RAN—in the Forest Stewardship Council (Carlton 2000). By contrast, in the case of privacy, advocacy groups such as EPIC and Privacy International flatly oppose self-regulation, and partnerships are rare.

Political risks such as the threat of government action or transnational activism are most likely to lead to self-regulatory strategies when three other factors are favorable: reputation, economic competition, and learning. Industries in which reputation is a key factor for selling services and products and in hiring talented staff are the most vulnerable to activist pressure.[101] Commitment to the highest technical standards, business "best practices," and corporate responsibility (including everything from employment policies, philanthropy, environmental protection, human rights, and corruption) can enhance the reputation of a company with its customers, employees, business partners, and policy makers. In the information-rich environment we have today, business activities are increasingly transparent to those monitoring their behavior and reputation becomes a shorthand way of identifying high-quality operations.

Firms that sell directly to consumers are most likely to value their brand name reputation and seek to preserve or enhance it. Therefore, it is the big name companies that tend to lead in adopting corporate codes and other voluntary initiatives, as demonstrated in all three of the cases. In the labor case, the firms most often involved in voluntary initiatives are in the clothing, textile, footwear, carpet, toy, and sporting goods sectors—all consumer-oriented companies with brand names such as Disney, Mattel, and Levi Strauss. The environmental case also shows how reputation has become important to the private sector. Some companies market green products or build their reputation around sustainable practices, and thus the response from consumers is key. Others more distant from the consumer also value a general positive reputation to facilitate political and economic relationships. The value of reputation for the information industries is that if consumers do not trust the companies, then the companies will not get the information they need.

Voluntary standard setting is a logical industry response to the political strategies of advocacy groups. These initiatives respond to the immediate concerns of the public, they provide reputational benefits that become a sort of "ethical" competitive advantage, and they can lead to dialogue and even partnership between advocacy organizations and the corporate community. The labor standards case stands out from the others because of the long-standing role of unions in labor–management relations. Union leaders have been only cautiously supportive of the corporate codes movement, because they are concerned that these codes could sidestep traditional collective bargaining and labor–management relations. In the U.S. AIP, the unionization issue divided the participants and drove out the union representatives. Human rights groups and other worker advocacy representatives were more willing to stay in the process, at least for now.

The economic risks involved in adopting self-regulatory programs clearly weigh heavily in the minds of many business leaders. Competitive pressures may create a reluctance to be out in front on corporate social responsibility. Although there is little clear evidence that the touted race to the bottom has occurred, there also is little clear evidence that a race to the top has become common.[102] In the environmental case, worries about being undercut in international competition or burdened with high costs have been used as an excuse for not adopting voluntary initiatives. But sustainability can provide a competitive advantage in some cases. Eco-efficiency can reduce costs by limiting wastes.[103] Green products and technologies can be used to build new markets. Common standards such as ISO 14000 can become the price of entry in some markets. And, most important, collective efforts such as Responsible Care take away some of the risk of being undercut by competitors.[104] If firms compete on cost alone, then there is a high probability that standards will not be upheld, or that firms with higher standards will be undercut by their rivals. If firms compete in part on quality, then raising standards becomes more likely. In general, once a firm adopts high standards, it has an incentive to ensure that as many others join as possible.

In each of the three issue areas, the mix of cost versus quality considerations in economic competition is different. Many people make a compelling case that pursuing ecologically sound business practices is also sound business, because it can increase efficiency and lead to the development of new technologies and new markets. Not all firms are convinced of these competitive advantages, but many are. A similar case is more difficult to make for labor standards. Few have made a compelling argument that raising worker standards will contribute to competitiveness and profitability, although that argument certainly could be made. The information industry case is particularly interesting, because two contradictory arguments have been put forward. A firm could be highly trusted by the public because it adheres to high standards of information privacy and gives each individual a choice about how their personal information will be used, which leads consumers to favor that firm over others. Widespread trust of this sort is viewed by many as a prerequisite for all sorts of new commercial markets to emerge in the information industries. All the same, commercial vendors who ask consumers for information have an incentive to avoid giving them a choice on how it is used, because consumers may choose not to have that information used in any way at all, which would kill that market.

The value of reputation to a wide variety of firms in a variety of political situations, and competition based on quality rather than cost, are two ideas that management has to learn and relearn. In all three cases, business elites—and the public—underwent a learning process that helped reinforce the idea that self-regulation might be an appropriate strategy to address real political problems. Many organizations now exist to educate the business community about sustainable business practices, books and journals regularly make the case for corporate environmentalism, and business schools now regularly teach courses on this topic. This has not been equally true in the case of labor standards, because there has not been the same persuasive case made, at least not in economic terms. Most labor activists try to convince business to adopt voluntary standards on moral grounds. The groups promoting privacy codes have had to engage in an intensive education campaign of both business and the public. A recent survey of 100 of Europe's leading business analysts and decision makers from France, Germany, and the United Kingdom revealed that corporate social and environmental responsibility is no longer viewed as an option but as a requirement for doing business (ENN 2000).

The leadership of key executives has been critical to the adoption of particular voluntary standards. The top leadership in a company has to believe in the value of these initiatives for them to have any real meaning. John Browne of BP Amoco publicly speaks out on issues of corporate social and environmental responsibility and has taken the company in a new direction on climate change, actively supporting the Kyoto Protocol. Business executives at Levi Strauss have been dedicated to maintaining good relations with workers for many years and took the lead in extending this to the company's suppliers around the world. It is more difficult to identify a similar corporate executive on information privacy issues, although the independent consultant and computer guru Esther Dyson has had significant influence on self-regulatory efforts in the information sector. The "moral first mover" gets others on board and can potentially institutionalize voluntary standards through what amounts to a "moral oligopoly," or a regime centered on corporate social purpose (Bobrowsky 1999). As one observer noted, "Corporate leaders have more credibility than any other group in American society to raise questions about the corporation" (Derber 1998, 231). In all three cases, the spread of information, education, and persuasion reinforced the idea that self-regulation would be a positive step toward reducing political risks, while potentially increasing economic benefits and meeting moral demands.

This discussion to some extent assumes that corporate leaders are driven to adopt self-regulation out of self-interest and that they do so sincerely. There is an alternative interpretation of the corporate codes movement, one common in the press: in the eyes of many observers, the increase in industry self-regulation is all about power and public relations. They believe that corporate leaders cynically adopt corporate codes either because it will make them look good without requiring any real change, or because it is one more way to demonstrate corporate power. It is certainly true that some companies initially thought they could put pretty words on paper, publicize it as a demonstration of their corporate responsibility, and then be granted more political leeway by governments and activist groups so that they could pursue their interests unhindered. It is also true that even good companies can do bad things (Schwartz and Gibb 1999). But is all this talk of self-regulation and corporate social responsibility really just that—talk? Or has it changed behavior in real ways?

Industry self-regulation has indeed changed some behavior, incrementally and unevenly. The evidence is scattered and difficult to analyze systematically. But firms such as Nike and Reebok do pay their workers in Vietnam more today than they did a few years ago. Companies such as BP Amoco and Shell have reduced their emissions of greenhouse gases and pollutants in measurable ways. IBM no longer advertises on web sites that do not have a certified privacy policy. But these changes are neither profound nor revolutionary, and in many cases they occur only at the margins.

The difficulty is in defining a single company or industry as altogether "good" or "bad." The same company that improves the conditions of workers in Vietnam may not do the same in Guatemala. The same company that cleans up five factories may not clean up the other twenty it owns. The same company that upholds high privacy standards for its web site may not do the same for its software. An industry association that establishes high standards for its members may not punish violators but may instead simply try to persuade and educate them. Abusive corporate practices remain at the heart of many contemporary debates about the relationship between the private sector and society.[105] The tobacco industry, for instance, has been revealed to be as corrupt as most people always suspected. The pharmaceuticals industry has been more concerned with maintaining its most profitable markets than in saving lives in the AIDS crisis in Africa. These and other behaviors that go against public expectations about appropriate conduct by the private sector illustrate the limits of self-regulation. They do not, however, demonstrate that these efforts should be abandoned altogether. Internal management systems that take account of the "triple bottom line" of performance (financial, social, environmental), auditing to global standards, and public reporting—all of which are becoming more common—require much more of a company than well-meaning words.

At the same time, there is no denying that MNCs are politically powerful, and that the growth in industry self-regulation is one more demonstration of that fact. Decades ago, John Kenneth Galbraith warned of the need for countervailing power against private interests, and many observers argue that today we no longer have the same constraints as in the past (Galbraith 1952). However, as the discussion of industry self-regulation demonstrates, MNCs are not completely unconstrained actors. They are held in check by transnational mobilization and by government intervention. Without some such countervailing power, effective self-regulation is unlikely.

The Challenges of Industry Self-Regulation

Industry self-regulation is, on the whole, a positive development. At the same time, it is not an unalloyed blessing for governments. The need for industry self-regulation reveals the gaps in global governance, where the profound lack of international consensus on important contemporary issues leaves them unresolved. Governments will have to consider how self-regulation affects domestic regulatory capacity, because it may conflict with public policy. On the one hand, if a government relies on voluntary initiatives to implement policy then it should certainly lower the cost of influencing and monitoring business behavior. Voluntary initiatives challenge governments to develop new institutional incentives for the private sector to expand these activities. On the other hand, these initiatives probably will not relieve the pressure on government to regulate in cases where the implementation of the codes is inadequate. The industrialized countries may view these voluntary private sector initiatives as a way to resolve the tensions between promoting foreign investment and high standards abroad at the same time. But these initiatives may also simply reflect the decreasing ability of governments to regulate domestically, or their unwillingness to negotiate international agreements restraining the behavior of MNCs. The international integration of markets has changed the ability and willingness of states to intervene in economic affairs, or at least, in the affairs of MNCs. Industry self-regulation can appear to be an abdication of government responsibility, and, if so, could actually undermine support for further globalization.

Voluntary action by industry is particularly challenging in North-South relations. From one perspective, it could be viewed as a way for the North to pursue protectionist policies to keep products from the South out of world markets. If major buyers require their suppliers to raise wages and improve working conditions, then factories that cannot or will not meet those conditions will be excluded from export markets. Some express concern that industry standards, once in place, will be adopted into international law, particularly under the WTO, thus enshrining the preferences of the private sector. From another perspective, industry self-regulation can be used to raise standards in developing countries and transfer best industry practices in a positive manner. Developing country governments generally welcome ISO 14000, for instance, because as local facilities become certified they will then be more likely to be able to sell in global markets. Developing country governments may also welcome the promotion of industry self-regulation if the only alternative is to incorporate these standards into strong international trade agreements.

There is no genuine consensus over how to raise standards around the world, and there is much concern that industry should not decide something so important. Despite the existence of many international guidelines, frameworks, and codes, how to implement them on the ground is not always clear. In many cases, the codes developed through negotiations between states, such as the ILO conventions, are more aspirational than real. Conflict between the interests of Northern and Southern governments will not be resolved through industry self-regulation, and in fact it could be exacerbated. This is particularly true in the case of labor issues, which are at the heart of national sociopolitical systems. If a company is under pressure from activists and its home government to facilitate, for instance, the freedom of association among its workers, then that company may come into direct conflict with the local political system. For instance, the Chinese government outlaws unions. Foreign businesses perhaps can speak out against this, but they cannot do anything directly to promote organizing without being viewed as subversive. Whether or not we want that system to be subverted, it is not clear that we should want the private sector to make that decision. The real need in this case is for the Chinese political system to change, which is beyond the scope of traditional business operations and legitimate action.

For governments that want to promote higher standards in the developing world, what are the alternatives? Sanctions have been a preferred policy in the United States to punish countries that violate accepted standards of behavior. But these sanctions often harm the very people they aim to protect, they have a poor record of effectiveness, they are costly to administer for both the public and private sectors, and they are not always the most appropriate policy to pursue. They are simply overkill in many situations. Industry self-regulation has become common precisely because it can be so difficult to change the policies of foreign governments. Another alternative is to negotiate binding international agreements. This is, in fact, the most common route today when it comes to environmental issues. But such negotiations are difficult, divisive, and often lead to inflexible rules that do not achieve their aims. International regulation by states may be no more effective in some cases than voluntary industry self-regulation (Chayes and Chayes 1998). A third alternative would be to promote rising standards abroad through extending carrots instead of sticks—by providing more foreign aid and technical assistance to raise general levels of economic development and increase local government capacity to govern effectively. This is a long-term project with uncertain dividends in the relatively distant future.

Governments can also find ways to leverage the private sector to promote its policy goals. They can promote industry self-regulation by using carrots and sticks—threatening regulation and providing incentives for self-regulation. For instance, in the climate change debate, early action by industry would be more likely if governments appear willing to give them credit in future climate change mitigation efforts. Governments can also promote corporate codes by facilitating consumer and shareholder activism, including rules about the treatment of shareholder resolutions, making it easy for activists to obtain information about corporate activities, and through the persuasive powers of government authorities. Policy makers can work to pass national and international legislation to require more public reporting by companies. Ultimately, public authorities may have a larger role to play in monitoring and certification systems, to ensure that they produce public labeling that is trustworthy and adheres to common standards. Many industry players complain of the proliferation of certifications and argue in favor of government action to harmonize all the different systems, from ISO 14000 to SA 8000 and on to all the other systems in existence.[106] If an international legal framework is devised that is performance-based instead of solely oriented to using a particular form of remediation, then industry will likely be more supportive and innovative. Partnerships between governments and the private sector can be a new tool in diplomacy. Social democrats in Europe and the United States are experimenting with corporate social responsibility as part of their "third way" policies, promoting free trade and free markets along with a social safety net that extends abroad. Multistakeholder processes for resolving international problems also have become increasingly common (Reinicke 1997; Nelson and Zadek n.d.)

The private sector, too, will find creating and maintaining self-regulatory initiatives to be a major challenge in the twenty-first century. Even the best corporate codes can be difficult to implement on the ground, often with unexpected side effects. Providing improved working conditions for a local community may skew the distribution of economic benefits within a country and lead to political divisions between the local and central governments, which may create new problems for the corporation. In countries intent on economic development, foreign investors may find little local support for investing in ecologically sustainable practices. In the context of global competition, individual industry players will continue to be tempted to defect from their commitment to self-regulate if the opportunity arises. Corporations strategically choose among alternative policies that include opting for national or international regulation over self-regulation or simply risking their reputation in pursuit of a big economic pay-off. But adopting corporate codes of conduct can also make it less costly and easier to cooperate with other companies in pursuing common ends. The difficulties of maintaining and extending these programs are complicated by the varying interests within the private sector, which is not some monolithic entity. Small companies have different interests than large ones, the extractive sector has different interests than the services sector, and companies based in different countries operate in often quite different ways.

One of the biggest challenges facing businesses attempting to implement voluntary programs is the organization of production itself. The extent of outsourcing makes business control of political and social conditions extremely difficult. Critics argue that outsourcing production to long supply chains encourages a race to the bottom among companies and puts great power in the hands of mostly Northern-based buyers. Others argue that outsourcing production leads to foreign investment in developing countries, transfer of technology, and economic development. The debate over outsourcing raises questions about the scope of control in modern firms and links organizational features with an array of social and political effects. The only certain solutions to the problems raised by outsourcing are either to have national enforcement of internationally accepted standards, or to stop the practice of outsourcing entirely. The former is only slightly more likely than the latter.

The widespread adoption of outsourcing and network forms of business organization makes monitoring systems central to effective voluntary standard setting. Monitoring raises all sorts of conflicting questions about who should do the monitoring, how it should be done and how often, and how to convey the results of monitoring to the wider public. Should it be performed internally, or done by an external auditor? Should those auditors be commercial firms, or should they be nonprofit groups with representatives from a variety of interests? Should monitoring be conducted by groups based in the developed world, or ones that come from the local community in which the business operates? Corporate executives tend to be deeply suspicious of any outside monitoring or auditing that involves advocacy groups, because they do not trust advocacy groups to be neutral in their assessments. They also worry about protecting trade secrets, especially in highly competitive markets. Public interest groups are equally suspicious that commercial auditors will not jeopardize their relations with major clients by turning in a critical report. Many Northern-based advocacy groups are also suspicious that local groups in developing countries do not know their own interests and are simply co-opted by the company or pressured by local government. International organizations may have some role to play, but they generally do not have sufficient resources to monitor on a large scale. Professional accounting and auditing firms may in fact be the most appropriate alternative, although this then also raises issues of training, certification, and expertise.

Another issue that will continue to confront companies adopting these programs is how to measure success. Many corporate critics establish absolute standards and expectations and cry foul when those are not met. Within the business community, in contrast, the goal often is to benchmark their behavior against other companies and against past performance. There is also disagreement over process versus outcomes in evaluating self-regulatory initiatives. This difference in perspective causes many observers to view self-regulation as weak and illegitimate. Variations and inconsistency in the monitoring, enforcement, and content of codes create problems of credibility and accountability. Most self-regulatory programs rely on persuasion and education instead of strict enforcement mechanisms, which opens them to further criticism, perhaps unjustified. These problems may be overcome as management systems for implementation such as ISO 14000 and SA 8000 improve and are more widely adopted. Public reporting also is a critical development, as increased transparency of corporate activity will reinforce the incentives for companies to adopt self-regulatory strategies. The Global Reporting Initiative has the potential to become a potent tool in influencing corporate behavior (GRI 2000).

The most difficult issue raised by self-regulation is accountability.

If a regulatory system is supposed to meet public goals, how does the public have any voice in a privately run system? In some sense, transnational activists have taken on the role of public voice by pressuring corporations to uphold particular standards. However, the most active advocacy organizations are not necessarily representative of the wider population; they are just the most vocal and well organized. Representative governments can and do have some voice in self-regulatory systems. In the case of information privacy, the United States and EU have been actively working with business to solve the problem of privacy protection. The main accountability mechanism comes down to the threat of government regulation, ending industry self-regulation, or at least limiting it. In all three cases discussed here, the problems that arise are largely because of the lack of effective national regulatory systems rather than solely due to corporate irresponsibility.

Initially, in many cases, advocacy groups developed their own set of standards to which they wanted corporations to be held, and businesses individually developed their own unique corporate codes of conduct. Over time the two sides have become remarkably more willing to work together on issues of common concern. The environmental community has taken the lead in pursuing these sorts of dialogues and partnerships, and the human rights community is beginning to participate with business in a way it would not have ten years ago. The result is that many voluntary standard-setting efforts are developed cooperatively by groups of industry and NGO representatives. We are still in the early stages of developing "ground rules" for interaction between the private sector and its critics, however. But one way to ensure the legitimacy of private sector standard setting is to make sure the process of developing and implementing standards is a shared endeavor among business, NGOs, and representative institutions.

If the kind of standard-setting activity represented in these three cases becomes widespread, then they will present new challenges to all the participants. Private sector self-regulation clearly poses new challenges for NGOs. To the degree that voluntary initiatives actually raise standards, the business community will expect to suffer less criticism from these groups. NGOs will need to publicize good behavior instead of concentrating their attention on highlighting the bad. But the low level of trust between most NGOs and the business community does not bode well. Some NGOs may be willing to engage in dialogue and form partnerships for specific projects, but they may not be able to sustain a long-term relationship. Many self-regulatory efforts probably will not meet all the criteria of all the many interested groups. Implementation systems may remain weak. The perceived failures of these exercises will tempt many NGOs to return to their former tactics—highlighting the violations of businesses and lobbying government for strict regulation.

The corporate community cannot look upon voluntary initiatives as the end of the game. As one observer describes the current context: "In this Renaissance-like situation of conflict, change and innovation there is no process to describe unequivocally what is right for companies operating internationally. No code of conduct can offer companies a 'safe haven' from all ethical choices" (Mitchell 1998, 2). Business self-regulation, by undermining support for government action on pressing public issues, may in turn place unrealistic expectations on the private sector. MNCs may have acquired some authority from a number of important resources they hold, such as information, expertise, benefits to distribute, and costs to impose, but they are increasingly viewed with suspicion by the public and need to tread warily (Gladwin and Walter 1980, 71). "Code fatigue" has already set in among some firms, and they will be tempted to return to old ways of doing business and dealing with the public. Self-regulatory initiatives require corporations to be much more open about their operations than before, and many find it difficult to accept this as the cost of doing business today. Engagement and transparency are essential for successful, legitimate, industry self-regulation—but they go against the status quo within both the business and the advocacy communities.

Industry Self-Regulation and Global Governance

Two items illustrate the changing nature of global governance. First, media mogul Ted Turner facilitated a deal between the United States and the United Nations in 2000 over the payment of U.S. dues by contributing $35 million to cover a projected one-year shortfall. Second, the Jubilee Movement, a coalition of groups representing religious, human rights, development, and other advocates, has persuaded numerous wealthy countries and the World Bank to forgive the debt of many of the poorest nations of the world. The character of international relations has changed in the past 50 years from one in which the global agenda was established by the most powerful countries, to one in which powerful commercial and activist groups shape the debate and often determine outcomes. Industry self-regulation is just one more piece of evidence regarding the changing nature of efforts to govern the global economy and establish collective mechanisms for resolving global policy issues.

This discussion of industry self-regulation has in general been couched in terms of corporate social responsibility. For its advocates, corporate social responsibility represents an attempt to shift the understanding of basic values in a capitalist system. It is idealistic and perhaps threatens to raise false hopes (Derber 1998, 228). But, as has been the case historically, private sector experimentation in developing and implementing standards and rules can create the basis for social consensus, which is the foundation upon which more appropriate regulation can be built. The problems that self-regulation attempts to address are often problems of national governance, and it is there that most responsibility still rests. Not surprisingly, industry self-regulation seems to work best within political systems that encourage it, and it works poorly when the political system works against it. In the past few decades, we have seen the emergence of a complex, multilayered system of global governance. Civil society "regulates" through its monitoring and advocacy functions. Industry regulates by setting standards for itself. Governments still do traditional governance, but governance now operates at local, national, and regional levels. A variety of international organizations now exist to deal with common problems among countries.

There are—and should be—limits to the role of business in designing policy. At a practical level, there are economies of scale in regulation by governments and international organizations. Industry self-regulation works most effectively when there is some legal recourse. The problems of labor in the developing world, for instance, cannot be resolved entirely by business because the real issue is the lack of recourse in weak or politically repressive regimes. Most important,

industry initiatives are not part of a political process in which accountability, equity, and participation are valued. What is good for a
large corporation is not necessarily good for a particular country or for
society in general.

Ultimately, much of the responsibility for resolving social problems in an accountable and democratic manner rests with governments. Democratic governments need to set minimum standards, appropriate to the level of development of the state and in accordance
with widely held values. Citizens must be empowered to determine
their own fate through democratic political processes. Values cannot
be imposed from abroad, from foreign activists, governments, or corporations. International industry self-regulation has the potential to
encourage significant improvements but only in concert with traditional political processes.

Notes

Introduction, notes 1–4

1. One of the main criticisms of the MAI was that it would have enshrined corporate rights in international law while ignoring corporate responsibilities. Following the end of the MAI negotiations, the Organization for Economic Cooperation and Development (OECD) revised and adopted a much weaker set of "guidelines" for national governments overseeing the behavior of MNCs.
2. The race to the bottom in regulatory policy among countries is so far not supported by systematic evidence (Drezner 2000). For an industry viewpoint on this debate, see the recent Business Roundtable report that argues that "U.S. companies with operations in China are contributing to the improvement of social, labor, and environmental conditions in China" (Business Roundtable 2000).
3. The *third way* is a term adopted by market-oriented parties of the center-left, especially in the United Kingdom and the United States. It has come to be associated with the policies of the Blair and Clinton regimes. For an explanation of this approach and a defense against critics, see Giddens (2000).
4. The failure of the MAI can be viewed as evidence of this weakness, although the subsequent success in revising the OECD Guidelines on Multinational Enterprises could be viewed as the opposite.

Chapter 1, notes 5–36

5. This view holds for developing and developed countries alike. In the United States, for instance, media attention highlights the perceived power of business to get its way in policy debates by wielding its financial

clout by contributing money to political campaigns. Mark Smith, in a recent analysis, disputes this, finding that business in the United States often loses politically unless it has public backing (Smith 2000).

6. Under the General Agreement on Tariffs and Trade (GATT) definitions, if it is voluntary, then it is labeled "standards." Some business representatives object to the term *self-regulation* because it makes them nervous about the possibility of government regulation, and they prefer to emphasize the voluntary nature of these efforts. Others applaud the term and argue that self-regulation by business is a more efficient and sophisticated mode of modern regulation, in contrast to traditional approaches.

7. A regulation is "a principle, rule, or law designed for controlling or governing behavior" (Riverside Publishing Company 1984, 990).

8. A business best practice is a "deliberate pattern of business activity that accomplishes its objective with outstanding efficiency and effectiveness, and contributes to exceptional performance," according to Paul O. Pederson of Price Waterhouse (Nelson 1996, 274). Business executives are becoming accustomed to the use of best practice models against which to measure their own organizational practices.

9. A technical distinction is often made between multinational corporations (MNCs) and transnational corporations (TNCs). An MNC is a corporation with complete production facilities located in different countries. A TNC is a corporation that locates different parts of the production process around the globe, for instance, producing all auto engines in one place, all auto bodies in another, and assembling it in a third location. The two terms are often used interchangeably, however. MNC will be preferred throughout this text, except when referring to UN documents and activities where TNC is the preferred usage.

10. A recent report by the OECD on investment trends emphasizes that foreign operations are no longer limited to the largest companies. Small- and medium-sized enterprises, including those from non-OECD countries, also participate in international markets (Thomson 2000).

11. For an excellent examination of these issues in the context of U.S.–EU relations, see Egan (1998).

12. Philip Cerny argues that the modern state is a "competition state," one that operates as another market player. The competition state does not simply deregulate in all policy areas, choosing instead to re-regulate but in more market-friendly ways (Cerny 1990; see also Aman 1995; Vogel 1996).

13. The actual size of governments measured in terms of revenue has not declined, despite more than a decade of supposed downsizing (World Bank 1997).

14. After the debacle of the failed MAI and the collapse of the Seattle talks on further multilateral trade negotiations, many leading policy makers talk about the need to soften the edges of globalization. UN Secretary-General Kofi Annan, in the Global Compact with business launched by

the United Nations, argues that globalization may be turned back if corporations that benefit from liberalization do not take account of the social effects of their activities. See Kell and Ruggie (1999).

15. Business executives look on this as affecting their "license to operate." Few firms actually do have their license to operate officially revoked by the government, although there are cases in which companies or their employees have been thrown out of a country. But anything that makes it too difficult for them to conduct normal business activities essentially takes away that license through informal means. There are some legal activists who argue that the United States should return to chartering companies publicly, and revoking those charters when the company violates community standards (Grossman and Adams 1993).

16. Going somewhat against this tide is Germany, where recent changes in law and society are producing a more Anglo-Saxon shareholder model of corporate governance. In Eastern Europe, demands for corporate social responsibility collide with the effort to dismantle the old communist system. Recent international discussions of corporate governance under the auspices of the OECD take a traditional view of corporate governance, defining it as the relationships among management, shareholders, and employees alone. But the final report on this topic acknowledged the existence of a more expansive definition of corporate obligations that reflects the permeation of stakeholder ideas into the mainstream (Millstein and Business Sector Advisory Group on Corporate Governance 1998).

17. Many U.S. companies hired ethics officers in response to changes in U.S. law, including sentencing guidelines that reduce penalties for companies and their officers if they have tried in good faith to prevent criminal conduct by employees. In many cases, these officers have also become responsible for broader issues of corporate social responsibility.

18. The International Organization for Standardization (ISO) is an international body made up of national standards associations. ISO 14000 lays out standards for an organizational process to implement an environmental code, although it does not set the content of the code itself.

19. The International Chamber of Commerce (ICC) put forward the first international codes addressing corporate behavior in the 1930s, covering advertising and marketing practices. The ICC also developed an International Code of Fair Treatment for Foreign Investment after World War II, which it intended to influence government policy toward MNCs.

20. Transfer pricing occurs when an MNC manipulates sales prices as goods and services are "sold" from one subsidiary or branch of the company to another, usually to minimize or evade taxes.

21. In the years following the failure of UN efforts, a number of states and nonstate actors negotiated narrowly tailored agreements regulating corporate behavior in specific sectors and on specific issues (Kline 1985). The most prominent of these were the World Health Organization (WHO)

code on marketing infant formula in developing countries and the Food and Agriculture Organization (FAO) Codex Alimentarius for food safety. These clearly never were intended to be comprehensive regulations of corporate behavior.

22. In 1984, the Irish National Caucus in the United States developed the MacBride Principles for U.S. companies in Northern Ireland. The principles state that company employment practices should not discriminate against anyone on the basis of religion. Unlike the Sullivan Principles, they were not international in scope. Public support for the MacBride Principles has reached extraordinary levels. Sixteen states and over 40 cities have passed legislation upholding the principles, and some city pension funds, including New York, do not invest in companies that do not adhere to them. Such well-known individuals as Jesse Jackson, Bob Dole, President Clinton, New York State Governor George Pataki, and New York City Mayor Rudolph Giuliani have all voiced support for the principles. Companies adopting them include AT&T, Dupont, Federal Express, GM, 3M, Phillip Morris, and Viacom.

23. The MAI collapsed under the weight of many competing interests among governments and not just because of the sudden mobilization of NGO opponents. Despite this, the anti-MAI story has been added as one more example of the strength of transnational activism today.

24. In practical use, the category of political risk has been quite elastic. For instance, the insurance industry has over time redefined what it considers a political risk in response to changes in politics and technology, and in what the industry was willing to insure (Haufler 1997; Moran 1999).

25. Jordana Friedman, Director of the International Security Program of the Council on Economic Priorities, pointed out that we need to develop good quantitative evidence that conflict management benefits the private sector, given that there is so much evidence of their potential indifference to conflict (Friedman 2000).

26. The pre-existing regulatory framework plays a role in determining regulatory risk in each case. The laws and regulations already on the books provide a template—sometimes a straitjacket—for thinking about regulatory change in particular policy domains. The information privacy case is interesting in part because cyberspace is an entirely new arena, a blank slate upon which old models and new are being tried.

27. According to the UN Conference on Trade and Development (UNCTAD), the number of companies that can be labeled "transnational" is still only a handful, although it is growing steadily (UNCTAD 2000).

28. The Montreal Protocol was negotiated in 1987 and revised in 1990 and 1992. The Convention on the Prohibition of the Development, Production, Stockpiling, and Use of Chemical Weapons and on their Destruction was opened for signature in 1992 and came into force in 1997.

29. The new OECD Guidelines are still voluntary, but 29 OECD governments plus four non-OECD governments have agreed to adopt them. They require each country to establish a national contact point where complaints can be lodged. It is still too early to tell whether this will be an effective constraint on international corporate behavior (Aaronson 2000).

30. There actually are three main strategies for SRI: screening, shareholder advocacy, and community-based investment. Numerous research reports in the past few years have shown that SRI does not necessarily conflict with profits, as many SRI funds outperformed nonscreened portfolios (Social Investment Forum 2000).

31. The legal frameworks in the United States and United Kingdom have meant that SRI takes different forms. The U.S. system allows and facilitates shareholder activism by only requiring 2 percent of eligible shareholders to sign on to file a proxy resolution. In much of Europe, proxy resolutions are impossible. In the United Kingdom, Canada, and Australia, SRI consists primarily of screening and advocacy/dialogue with company management (Oxford Analytica 2000).

32. The contributions of asset specificity to the organization of market activity have been explored theoretically by Oliver Williamson (1985).

33. The literature on the "obsolescing bargain" between a MNC and its host country provides evidence that over time the host government gains more leverage in the relationship, and "creeping regulation" is likely. This may also be true, to a certain degree, for some manufacturing industries but not for supply chain relations (Kobrin 1987).

34. The saga of Microsoft and its erstwhile partners, now suing it for antitrust violations, provides a cautionary tale about the value of a reputation as a responsible and trustworthy partner. Despite the fact that Microsoft did not have a good reputation, many firms sought partnerships with it for competitive reasons. A positive reputation can facilitate a business relationship, but competitive advantage is even more important.

35. The discussion within the business community on these issues is framed in terms of "corporate citizenship," "corporate social responsibility," and "business ethics." It is not referred to as self-regulation except in the case of information privacy.

36. Almost all UN agencies are now actively pursuing partnerships with business. The most prominent is the Global Compact, but the most controversial in some ways is the recently ended private sector program of the UN Development Program (UNDP). This program consisted of a handful of large MNCs that contributed funds and expertise to a major campaign to support market-oriented development projects. Many people criticized the UNDP for selling out to business interests and jeopardizing genuine development in favor of capitalist profit making.

Chapter 2, notes 37–55

37. The degree of environmental regulation and its effectiveness of course varies considerably across countries (Jaenicke and Weidner 1997; Schreurs and Economy 1997; Clark et al. 2001).

38. These disasters often provide lessons to *others* but not to the original corporate offender; for instance, Exxon itself is not a leader in corporate social responsibility although other oil companies are.

39. There are conflicting reports of exactly how many people were killed or injured, although all agree it was in the thousands. For instance, the Corporate Watch web site <http://www.corpwatch.org/trac/bhopal> lists 8,000 killed and 500,000 injured, while a web site by Union Carbide <http://www.bhopal.com> reports that 3,800 died and over 3,000 were severely disabled from the accident.

40. For more information, see the excellent web site hosted by the Alaskan government <http://www.oilspill.state.ak.us>.

41. CERES stands for the Coalition for Environmentally Responsible Economies.

42. To allay company fears that the CERES commitments create a new liability, the principles themselves contain a disclaimer against holding a company legally responsible in court for adhering to them.

43. The U.S. government grew concerned that the EMS adopted in Great Britain and the EU could become a barrier to U.S. corporate competitiveness. They argued that the Europeans developed standards that would disadvantage the United States and feared they would vote as a bloc in other international forums on this issue. The ISO appeared the safest venue. Business interests supported the ISO because they had a strong voice in its deliberations (Haufler 1999).

44. The process leading to the development of ISO 14000 has been heavily criticized in the NGO community. Many NGOs and developing countries had very little input into the final product. One consultant views it as "missed opportunity" (Krut and Gleckman 1998). There is now an NGO Initiative on ISO 14000 to monitor continuing development and implementation of the standards (Ecologia 2000).

45. ISO 14000 is an interesting case of the blending of public and private regulation. Companies adopt the standards voluntarily. However, the governments of countries as diverse as Great Britain and Indonesia are beginning to write ISO certification into domestic legislation. Some developing countries welcome the ISO standards; they know they do not have the capacity to develop their own systems, and they hope that ISO certification will help their national companies become competitive in world markets.

46. Writing about the Canadian corporate codes movement, John English claims the public commitments made by BP galvanized interest among

Canadian environmentalists and business leaders in the extractive industries. "By 1998, placards were common, conferences on corporate social responsibility abounded, and shareholder activists bothered company presidents at annual meetings" (English 2000, 4).

47. The FSC has been criticized for being too soft on loggers. Some large U.S. timber companies find it too harsh and have attempted to set up a rival organization, the Sustainable Forestry Initiative (Carlton 2000).

48. This quotation is from a special newspaper series on how pharmaceutical companies use people in the developing world as test subjects for new drugs. It raises ethical concerns about whether the companies conduct these trials with fully informed consent from people who have a choice about whether to participate.

49. Recent protests in Seattle, Washington, D.C., and Prague demonstrate the effective organizational mobilization of diverse constituent groups.

50. In many cases, the real barrier to truly eco-efficient production is simply that it would require a huge investment to re-engineer the manufacturing process, with benefits in the long term but high start-up costs in the short term.

51. The Natural Step is a nonprofit environmental organization based in Sweden that promotes a framework for redesigning activities to be more ecologically sound. It is based on systems thinking and whole processes. According to its web site, more than 70 municipalities and 60 corporations have adopted their program, including IKEA, Electrolux, and McDonalds (The Natural Step 2000).

52. Haas, an academic expert on international environmental politics, notes the influence of new norms articulated by ecological "epistemic" (expert) communities. These norms are incorporated into formal institutions and also into more informal, nonstate based agencies, such as the business organizations discussed here (Haas 1999, 104).

53. GRI claims that some governments have inquired about adopting the GRI guidelines as part of official government programs (GRI 2000).

54. Most companies are not so forthcoming. Many executives resist revealing too much information, fearing it would be an open invitation to media attention and legal liability. Even if this fear is overcome, many firms simply do not have the relevant information easily available; few companies collect data on the myriad ways in which the company affects the environment. For example, when BP Amoco committed to reducing its emissions of greenhouse gases, it first had to find out how much it already emitted, which no one knew. Establishing this baseline required collecting data at all its individual facilities around the world.

55. Standards organizations support themselves by selling the standards; less developed countries often do not have the funds to buy them.

Chapter 3, notes 56–79

56. Ruggie refers to postwar welfare state policies as "embedded liberalism," in which the state promoted free trade and open markets at the same time that labor received rising wages, state-supplied welfare benefits, and steady employment (Ruggie 1983).

57. Total compensation includes direct hourly wages, benefits, and all other direct and indirect payments.

58. Analysts disagree about the effects of globalization on inequality. Williamson argues that globalization in the nineteenth century led to rising inequality in the richer countries and declining inequality in the poorer countries. He also asserts that globalization in the late twentieth century is having similar effects (Williamson 1997).

59. The top 100 TNCs are becoming increasingly transnationalized, when measured in terms of their assets, employment, and sales abroad compared to their total assets, employment, and sales. TNCs from developing countries also are becoming more transnationalized, even more rapidly than companies based in the industrialized countries. The most transnational sectors among the top 100 TNCs overall were food and beverages, chemicals and pharmaceuticals, and electronics and electrical equipment (UNCTAD 1998).

60. The largest employers in the world are Chinese state-owned firms.

61. The founders of the ILO saw it as a way to avoid a repeat of the Russian Revolution by raising living standards in an international process negotiated among business, labor, and government. The ILO has adopted numerous voluntary conventions, but few have been ratified by every member government. It has no enforcement powers but relies on monitoring, persuasion, and technical assistance to enhance the conditions of work around the globe.

62. The definition of a living wage is controversial. Generally, it refers to wages for a full-time worker that meet the needs of a family, raising it above poverty level and allowing a small amount of savings. Every element of this is contested—what size family to use as standard; what are basic needs; what is the poverty level; and how much surplus for savings is appropriate. Most corporations will commit to paying minimum wages but not living wages.

63. There are a number of causes for Nike's current financial weakness, and not all can be laid at the doorstep of anti-sweatshop attacks on it.

64. The boy, Craig Kielburger, later publicly lectured Prime Minister Jean Chretien on the need to link trade with human rights (English 2000).

65. The U.S. government persuaded the participants to negotiate, but it did not have a direct vote or seat at the table. Officials believed that any di-

rect participation would drive away business participants, who did not want this effort to have even a hint of regulation about it.

66. The launch of SA 8000 created a certain amount of controversy in the standards-setting community. An industry group, Industry Cooperation on Standards and Conformity Assessment, complained of the proliferation and high costs of the multiplicity of standards and certifications today, especially SA 8000. At a meeting in Munich in 1998, about 58 members put forth a "manifesto" in protest, arguing in favor of harmonization of standards and self-certification to lower costs (Zuckerman 1998a). One report on the launch of SA 8000 commented that it "stunned" the international standards community and directly challenged the preeminence of the ISO on international standards (Zuckerman 1998b).

67. The passage of the Declaration of Fundamental Principles spurred many countries to re-examine why they had not adopted the relevant conventions previously. This led in turn to a rash of ratifications in the past two years. Still, as of December 2000, only 22 countries have officially ratified all eight of the conventions that make up the Fundamental Principles.

68. Prior to the 1998 annual ILO conference, the Global March Against Child Labor traversed the world, ending in Geneva, to draw global attention to the worst forms of child labor. One year later, the ILO adopted a new ILO Convention Concerning the Prohibition and Immediate Elimination of the Worst Forms of Child Labor. This convention must be adopted and enforced by governments, and many have already made this commitment.

69. They included Harvard University, the University of Michigan, the University of Notre Dame, Ohio State University, and the University of California. After publication, the consultant went on to condemn the report as too weak.

70. Wal-Mart claims that it does not conduct business with Saipan factories, and there is some evidence to support that claim. The companies all say they follow U.S. law in hiring subcontractors, and Nordstrom promised to hire its own investigator.

71. The contrast between Canadian and U.S. business preferences in similar negotiations is striking. U.S. business clearly did not want official government participation or voting in the AIP. The Canadian business representatives, however, insisted that the government play a prominent role in the process (English 2000).

72. Jay Mazur, president of UNITE and Chair of the AFL-CIO International Affairs committee, has pointed out the danger that too eager support for voluntary codes could lead policy makers to view codes as a substitute for enforcement of existing laws, prevent adoption of new legislation, and further block the linkage of trade with labor standards (Mazur 2000).

73. The Canadian efforts also faced institutional barriers: labor issues in Canada are a provincial, not a federal, responsibility.

74. The two sides generally agreed on all the major subjects to be addressed in the code. On almost every one, however, they disagreed about what exactly to do (English 2000).

75. Nike hired a number of independent auditors, including former ambassador Andrew Young, to check its foreign subcontractors in Vietnam. When these audits came back with fairly positive results, many labor and human rights groups criticized the methodology and sent their own monitors to talk to factory workers and disprove the auditors' report.

76. The actual method for conducting social audits is still evolving. UNCTAD devotes resources and expertise to developing effective and usable social accounting systems that mimic the financial accounting with which the private sector is most comfortable.

77. Levi Strauss found itself under criticism on the home front, too. It had to shut down plants and restructure when its growth rate slowed and sales declined, thus throwing workers in Belgium and France out of their jobs. Levi Strauss was one of the last major U.S. apparel manufacturers to produce much of its product in-house, without extensive subcontracting to overseas factories, as noted in the *Financial Times*, February 23, 1999.

78. Some critics argue that such extensive supply chains are inefficient and inhuman. They argue that most products should be made closer to home and directly by company employees, to ensure more control and responsibility over such issues as worker standards.

79. Good data on such important issues as wage levels are very difficult to find in many countries. It can be difficult to determine what to include: Should it include overtime? Is that overtime mandatory or voluntary? Are there any regular costs that workers are forced to pay to the managers? Nevertheless, we can say with certainty that most workers in developing countries are paid extremely low wages compared to those in the industrialized world.

Chapter 4, notes 80–98

80. This is often referred to as business-to-business (B2B) commerce. B2B includes using online services to gather companies from around the world to aggregate their purchase orders, or to match buyers and sellers on a global scale, or to manage the supply chain of a networked company. This is still in its very early stages; for instance, one firm has laid out a multiyear roadmap for creating more than 120 standards in order to enable B2B in the electronics industry alone (Heck 2000). The growth of

B2B raises concerns not just about privacy but about antitrust and competition policy. See Federal Trade Commission Staff (2000).

81. One journalist writing on this topic cites a spring 1998 Business Week/ Harris Poll, which indicated that 59 percent of those polled would never provide a web site with registration information, and 97 percent were reluctant to share any personal information at all (Steer 1999).

82. For an interesting discussion of how the "new" economy is transforming the "old," see Rauch (2000).

83. One of the best introductions to this issue, and particularly the contrast between American and European approaches, can be found in Peter Swire and Robert Litan's *None of Your Business* (1998).

84. For example, U.S. sectoral regulation includes the Fair Credit Reporting Act, the Children's Online Privacy Act of 1998, the Electronic Funds Transfer Act, the Health Insurance Portability and Accountability Act of 1996, and others.

85. A number of states have regulations regarding financial, medical, and insurance data; bans on spamming; and other specific information privacy issues.

86. By 1998 twenty EU member states had ratified the convention.

87. Those who advocate giving individuals such property rights believe that personal information has become so valuable that it makes no sense to give it away for free. Therefore, each individual should be able to negotiate a price for selling data to information collecting entities. "As the cost of gathering, packaging and reselling information goes to zero, the most advantaged owner of information about the individual is the individual. That is, the customer can assemble more valuable information about him- or herself than any third party, and can profit accordingly" (Evans 1999).

88. The European Economic Area includes the fifteen members of the EU plus Iceland, Norway, and Liechtenstein.

89. Up until recently the new information players stayed away from Washington, believing they would prevail politically because of the vital importance of the information sector to the growth of the new economy. Giants such as Microsoft came late to the political game and only after an antitrust lawsuit brought the power of government to its attention.

90. One of the more extreme examples of this can be found in an article in *Wired* magazine ("Welcome to Sealand: Now Bugger Off"), which describes a group of computer geeks who plan to make an offshore platform into a computer hub. They want to give corporations and individuals the freedom "to store and move data without answering to anybody, including competitors, regulators, and lawyers" (Garfinkel 2000, 230). They have an initial investment of $1 million to launch the project.

91. The OPA White Paper on U.S. data privacy provides an excellent overview of these efforts (Blackmer and Charyton 1998).

92. The antitrust case against Microsoft has revealed much about the dynamics of industry competition and cooperation, hostility and partnership. See Heilemann (2000).

93. TRUSTe also incorporates the Fair Information Practices recommended by the U.S. Federal Trade Commission and Department of Commerce.

94. Some people fear that the same software technology that could provide consumers with more choice about how their personal data are used could also provide autocratic governments with a tool to ensure their own citizens do not have free access to the Internet.

95. A recent study claims that the level of consumer fear of privacy invasion is correlated with the rise in CNET online news coverage of the issue (Steer 1999).

96. The OPA represents a coalition of global companies and associations founded in 1998. Its members have agreed to abide by "meaningful" privacy standards—ones that are enforceable by government. The OPA also strongly supports private sector certification or seal programs.

97. The White House Task Force developed the framework, but other U.S. agencies have come to similar conclusions with regard to effective privacy protection.

98. The hot-button issue in Europe when it comes to privacy is the ECHELON intelligence collection system. This secret system, allegedly created by the United States with cooperation from Great Britain, Australia, New Zealand, and Canada, is rumored to be capable of capturing and analyzing telephone, facsimile, and e-mail transmissions, searching for specific keywords indicating terrorist or criminal activity. It is viewed suspiciously as "Big Brother," or perhaps "Big American Brother."

Chapter 5, notes 99–106

99. One study of environmental policy argues that companies have their greatest political influence when there are no negotiations over a formal, binding international regime governing the issue, because business leaders can then use their clout with national governments and international bureaucracies to protect their freedom of maneuver (Porter and Brown 1996, 63).

100. This report examined the innovative use of information technology by advocacy groups, from issue tracking to voter guides, interactive databases, resource files, news services, mobilization programs, and others. See Foundation for Public Affairs (2000).

101. For a more critical view of corporate reputation and how it affects relations between society and the private sector, see Klein (1999).

102. In general, most companies in the past decade have invested in countries with well-developed regulatory systems, such as Europe and the United States. Investment in developing countries usually leads to technology transfer and economic growth without weakening government regulatory capacity (Drezner 2000). But the possibility that competition among firms on the basis of quality will lead to a spiral of rising standards is only a possibility as yet, although the widespread adoption of certification standards such as ISO 14000 may lead to just that.

103. What is often termed an "industrial ecology" view can lead to innovations that improve efficiency, lower costs, and raise the value of products. For example, 3M claims it has saved over $700 million through its Pollution Prevention Pays Program. However, a corporation cannot concentrate all its attention on materials and energy use while neglecting other sources of competitiveness (Esty and Porter 1998).

104. Collective efforts, however, can suffer from the free rider problem unless members of the group can monitor one another's behavior and check any attempts to cheat (Bobrowsky 1999).

105. Many of the most prominent popular books on corporations focus on the ways in which corporations pursue profits at the expense of social goals (Korten 1995; Greider 1997; Mokhiber and Weissman 1999).

106. The Big Three automakers have their own quality assurance standards; the European Union has its EMAS for environmental management system standards; in addition, there is SA 8000, ISO 14000, and others (Zuckerman 1998a).

References

Aaronson, Susan. 2000. "The OECD Guidelines." Speech delivered at the New America Foundation, Washington, D.C., November 30.

Adams, Roger. 1998. *Linking Environmental and Financial Performance: A Survey of Best Practice Techniques.* Geneva: UNCTAD.

Aman, Alfred. 1995. "A Global Perspective on Current Regulatory Reforms: Rejection, Relocation, or Reinvention?" *Indiana Journal of Global Legal Studies,* vol. 2, no. 2, pp. 429–64.

———. 1999. "Administrative Law for a New Century," in *Globalization and Governance,* ed. Aseem Prakash and Jeffrey A. Hart. London and New York: Routledge.

Amon, Elizabeth. 2000. "Coming to America: Alien Tort Claims Act Provides a Legal Forum for the World." *National Law Journal,* vol. 23 (October), p. A1.

Banisar, David. 2000. *Privacy and Human Rights 2000: An International Survey of Laws and Developments.* London and Washington, D.C.: EPIC and Privacy International.

BBBOnline. 2000. Available at <www.bbbonline.org>.

Berger, Suzanne, and Ronald Dore. 1996. *National Diversity and Global Capitalism.* Ithaca, N.Y.: Cornell University Press.

Berman, Jonathan. 2000. "Boardrooms and Bombs: Strategies of Multinational Corporations in Conflict Areas." *Harvard International Review,* vol. XXII, no. 3 (Fall 2000).

Bessette, Rändi, and Virginia Haufler. 2001. "Against All Odds: Why There Is No International Information Regime." *International Studies Perspectives,* vol. 2, pp. 69–92.

Birdsall, Nancy. 1998. "Life is Unfair: Inequality in the World." *Foreign Policy,* no. 111, pp. 76–94.

Blackmer, W. Scott, and Lynn Charyton. 1998. OPA *White Paper: Online Consumer Data Privacy in the United States.* Washington, D.C.: Online Privacy Alliance.

Bobrowsky, David. 1999. "Corporate Governance Games and the Setting of Standards in the Global Economy." Paper presented at Annual Meeting of the International Studies Association, Washington, D.C., February 16–20.

Boyer, Robert, and Daniel Drache, eds. 1996. *States Against Markets: The Limits of Globalisation*. London: Routledge.

BP Amoco. 2000. *Annual Report*. London: BP Amoco.

Braudel, Fernand. 1981–1984. *Civilization and Capitalism, 15th–18th Century*. Vol. 3: The Perspectives of the World. Trans. Sian Reynolds. New York: Harper & Row.

Bray, John. 1999. *No Hiding Place*. London: Control Risks, Ltd.

Broad, Robin, and John Cavanagh. 1998. *The Corporate Accountability Movement: Lessons and Opportunities*. World Resources Institute, Washington, D.C., unpublished manuscript.

Buchan, David. 1998. "Multinationals Making Explicit Commitment." *Financial Times*, April 22.

Burke, Pamela. 1999. "Oil Companies and Indigenous Peoples in Ecuador," in *Private Authority and International Affairs*, ed. A. Claire Cutler, Virginia Haufler, and Tony Porter. Albany, N.Y.: State University of New York.

Business Ethics. 1999. Untitled. March/April, p. 6.

Business Roundtable. 2000. *Corporate Social Responsibility: Practices by U.S. Companies*. Washington, D.C.: Business Roundtable.

Carlton, Jim. 2000. "How Home Depot and Activists Joined to Cut Logging Abuse." *Wall Street Journal*, September 26.

Cerny, Philip G. 1990. *The Changing Architecture of Politics: Structure, Agency, and the Future of the State*. London: Sage Press.

Chayes, Abram, and Antonia Handler Chayes. 1998. *The New Sovereignty: Compliance with International Regulatory Agreements*. Cambridge, Mass.: Harvard University Press.

Chemical Market Reporter. 1999. "ISO 14000 Standards Gain Wider Acceptance as Companies Upgrade Their Operations According to International Environmental Standards." *Chemical Market Reporter*, vol. 255, no. 20, p. 12.

Clapp, Jennifer. 1998. "The Privatization of Global Environmental Governance: ISO 14000 and the Developing World." *Global Governance*, vol. 4, no. 3, pp. 295–316.

Clark, William C., Jill Jaeger, Josee van Eijndhoven, and Nancy M. Dickson, eds. 2001. *Social Learning Group 2001: Learning to Manage Global Environmental Risks: A Comparative History of Social Responses to Climate Change, Ozone Depletion, and Acid Rain*. Cambridge, Mass.: MIT Press.

Council of Europe. 1981. *Convention for the Protection of Individuals with Regard to Automatic Processing of Personal Data*. Strasbourg: Council of Europe.

———. 1989. *New Technologies: A Challenge to Privacy Protection?* Strasbourg: Council of Europe.

Cutler, A. Claire, Virginia Haufler, and Tony Porter, eds. 1999. *Private Authority and International Affairs.* SUNY Series in Global Politics. Albany, N.Y.: State University of New York.

Derber, Charles. 1998. *Corporation Nation: How Corporations Are Taking Over Our Lives and What We Can Do About It.* New York: St. Martin's Press.

DeYoung, Karen, and Deborah Nelson. 2000. "The Body Hunters: Latin America is Ripe for Trials, and Fraud." *Washington Post*, December 21, pp. A1, A18–19.

Doremus, Paul N., William W. Keller, Louis W. Pauly, and Simon Reich. 1998. *The Myth of the Global Corporation.* Princeton, N.J.: Princeton University Press.

Drake, William. 1999. *Toward Sustainable Competition in Global Telecommunications.* Washington, D.C.: Aspen Institute.

Drezner, Daniel. 2000. "Bottom Feeders." *Foreign Policy*, no. 121 (November–December), pp. 64–70.

Earth Rights International. 2000. "Total Denial Continues." Washington, D.C.: Earth Rights International.

Ecologia. 2000. *ISO 14000 NGO Initiative.* Available at <www.ecologia.org/iso14000/opcom/opcom.html>.

Egan, Michelle. 1998. *Mutual Recognition and Standard-Setting: Public and Private Strategies for Regulating Transatlantic Markets.* American Institute for Contemporary German Studies Seminar Papers/Policy Papers no. 10. Washington, D.C.: American Institute for Contemporary German Studies.

Elkington, John. 1998. *Cannibals with Forks: The Triple Bottom Line of 21st Century Business.* Stony Creek, Conn.: New Society Publishers.

English, John. 2000. *Negotiating a Code of Conduct: A Canadian Experience.* Paper presented at the conference on the Global Compact and UN Institutions, Tokyo, Japan, July 14–15.

Environmental News Networks (ENN). 2000. "Big Business Puts Environment in Its Big Picture." *Environmental News Networks.* Available on <www.enn.com/enn-news-archive/2000/06/06272000/envirosurvey_14227.asp>.

Esty, Daniel, and Michael Porter. 1998. "Industrial Ecology and Competitiveness: Strategic Implications for the Firm." *Journal of Industrial Ecology*, vol. 2, no. 1, pp. 35–43.

Ethics Officers Association. 2000. "Member Survey 2000." *EOA News*, vol. 2, no. 3, p. 1.

European Commission Data Protection Working Party. 1999. "Opinion 2/99 on the Adequacy of the 'International Safe Harbor Principles,' Issued by the U.S. Department of Commerce, 19 April 1999." Brussels: European Commission.

Evans, Phil. 1999. "Strategy and the New Economics of Information." *Financial Times–Mastering Information Management, Part Two*, February 8, pp. 2–4.

Federal Trade Commission Staff. 2000. *Entering the 21st Century: Competition Policy in the World of B2B Electronic Marketplaces*. Washington, D.C.: Federal Trade Commission.

Florini, Ann, ed. 2000. *The Third Force: The Rise of Transnational Civil Society*. Tokyo and Washington, D.C.: Japan Center for International Exchange and the Carnegie Endowment for International Peace.

Forest Stewardship Council United States. 2000. "About FSC." Available at <www.fscus.org/html/about_fsc/index.html>.

Fortune Magazine. 2000. "Fortune 500." Available at <www.fortune.com>.

Foundation for Public Affairs. 2000. *Cyber Activism: Advocacy Groups and the Internet*. Washington, D.C.: Foundation for Public Affairs.

Friedman, Jordana. 2000. Speech delivered at the Business and International Security Conference, International Peace Forum, New York City, April 29.

Galbraith, John Kenneth. 1952. *American Capitalism*. Boston: Houghton Mifflin.

Garcia-Johnson, Ronie. 2000. *Exporting Environmentalism: U.S. Multinational Chemical Corporations in Brazil and Mexico*. Cambridge, Mass.: MIT Press.

Garfinkel, Simson. 2000. "Welcome to Sealand: Now Bugger Off." *Wired*, vol. 8.07 (July), pp. 230–39.

Garrett, Geoffrey. 1998. *Partisan Politics in the Global Economy*. New York: Cambridge University Press.

General Motors. 2000. Company profile. Available at <www.gm.com>.

Georgetown University. 1999. *Georgetown Internet Privacy Policy Survey, Executive Summary*. Washington, D.C.: Georgetown University.

Giddens, Anthony. 2000. *The Third Way and Its Critics*. Cambridge, Mass.: Polity Press/ Blackwell Publishers.

Gladwin, Thomas N., and Ingo Walter. 1980. *Multinationals Under Fire: Lessons in the Management of Conflict*. New York: John Wiley & Sons.

Global Reporting Initiative (GRI). 2000. "Frequently Asked Questions, GRI." Available at <www.globalreporting.org>.

Gomes-Casseres, Benjamin. 1994. "Group Versus Group: How Alliance Networks Compete." *Harvard Business Review* (July–August), pp. 62–73.

Gordon, Kathryn. 1999. "Rules for the Global Economy: Synergies Between Voluntary and Binding Approaches." Paper presented at the Conference on Corporate Citizenship—Linking CSR Business Strategies and the Emerging International Agenda, Royal Institute of International Affairs, London, November 8–9.

Government of Canada. 1998. *Voluntary Codes: A Guide for their Development and Use*. Ottawa: Government of Canada.

Greider, William. 1997. *One World, Ready or Not: The Manic Logic of Global Capitalism.* New York: Touchstone/Simon and Schuster.

Grossman, Richard L., and Frank T. Adams. 1993. "Taking Care of Business: Citizenship and the Charter of Incorporation." *Earth Island Journal,* vol. 8, no. 2, pp. 34+.

Haas, Peter M. 1999. "Social Constructivism and the Evolution of Multilateral Environmental Governance," in *Globalization and Governance,* ed. Aseem Prakash and Jeffrey A. Hart. London and New York: Routledge.

Harrison, Kathryn. 1999. "Talking with the Donkey: Cooperative Approaches to Environmental Regulation." *Journal of Industrial Ecology,* vol. 2, no. 3, pp. 51–72.

Harverson, Patrick. 1999. "Clearing the Air." *Financial Times/Responsible Business,* June 30, p. 20.

Haufler, Virginia. 1997. *Dangerous Commerce: Insurance and the Management of International Risk.* Ithaca, N.Y.: Cornell University Press.

——. 1999. *Negotiating International Standards for Environmental Management Systems: The ISO 14000 Standards.* Global Public Policy Network. Washington, D.C., unpublished manuscript.

Hawken, Paul. 1993. *The Ecology of Commerce.* New York: HarperBusiness.

Hawken, Paul, Amory Lovins, and L. Hunter Lovins. 2000. *Natural Capitalism: Creating the Next Industrial Revolution.* New York: Little, Brown.

Heck, Stefan. 2000. "Debunking the Myths of B2B." *ZDNet.* Available at <www.zdnet.com/zdnn/stories/comment/0,5859,2641264.00.html>.

Heilemann, John. 2000. "The Truth the Whole Truth and Nothing but the Truth: The Untold Story of the Microsoft Antitrust Case." *Wired,* vol. 8, no. 11, pp. 260–311.

Hirst, Paul, and Grahame Thompson. 1995. *Globalisation in Question.* Cambridge, U.K.: Polity Press.

Hogarth, Sharon. 1999. "On the Horizon: ISO 14000." *Manufacturing Engineering,* vol. 122, no. 3, pp. 118–28.

Horovitz, Bruce. 2001. "Marketers Tout Consumer Privacy: Strategy Tackles Hot Button Issue." *USA Today,* March 1.

IBM. 1998. "Privacy in Play." Available at <www.ibm.com/ibm/thinkmag/articles/privacy/text.html>.

Independent University Initiative (2000). "Final Report." Produced by Business for Social Responsibility Education Fund, Investor Responsibility Research Center, and Dara O'Rourke. Cambridge, Mass.: Independent University Initiative.

Inglehart, Ronald. 1997. *Modernization and Postmodernization: Cultural, Economic, and Political Change in 43 Societies.* Princeton, N.J.: Princeton Paperbacks.

International Labor Organization (ILO). 1998. *World Employment Report 1996–97.* Geneva: ILO Publications

International Organization for Standardization (ISO). 2000. *The ISO Survey of ISO 9000 and ISO 14000 Certificates.* Geneva: ISO.

Investor Responsibility Research Center. 2000. "IRRC." Available at <www.irrc.org.>

Jaenicke, Martin, and Helmut Weidner, eds. 1997. *National Environmental Policies: A Comparative Study of Capacity-Building.* Berlin: Springer.

Jonge Oudraat, Chantal de, and P. J. Simmons. Forthcoming. *Managing Global Issues: Lessons Learned.* Washington, D.C.: Carnegie Endowment for International Peace.

Kapstein, Ethan. 1999. "Distributive Justice and International Trade." *Ethics and International Affairs,* vol. 13, pp. 175–204.

Keck, Margaret E., and Kathryn Sikkink. 1998. *Activists Beyond Borders: Advocacy Networks in International Politics.* Ithaca, N.Y.: Cornell University Press.

Kell, Georg, and John Gerard Ruggie. 1999. "Global Markets and Social Legitimacy: The Case of the 'Global Compact.'" Paper presented at conference on Governing the Public Domain beyond the Era of the Washington Consensus? Redrawing the Line between the State and Market, York University, Toronto, November 4–6.

Klein, Naomi. 1999. *No Logo: Taking Aim at the Brand Bullies.* New York: Picador Press.

Kline, John. 1985. *International Codes and Multinational Business: Setting Guidelines for International Business Operations.* Westport, Conn.: Quorum Books.

Klotz, Audie. 1995. *Norms in International Relations: The Struggle Against Apartheid.* Ithaca, N.Y.: Cornell University Press.

Kobrin, Stephen. 1987. "Testing the Bargaining Hypothesis in the Manufacturing Sector of Developing Countries." *International Organization,* vol. 41, no. 4, pp. 609–38.

Korten, David C. 1995. *When Corporations Rule the World.* West Hartford, Conn.: Kumarian Press.

KPMG. 2000. "KPMG Ethics Survey 2000." Available at <www.kpmg.ca/english/services/fas/publications/ethicssurvey2000.html>.

Krasner, Stephen. 1983. "Introduction," in *International Regimes,* ed. Stephen Krasner. Ithaca, N.Y.: Cornell University Press.

Krut, Riva and Harris Gleckman. 1998. *ISO 14001: A Missed Opportunity for Sustainable Global Industrial Development.* London: Earthscan Publications Ltd.

Kyloh, Robert, ed. 1998. *Mastering the Challenge of Globalization: Towards a Trade Union Agenda.* Geneva: International Labor Office.

Leggett, Jeremy, ed. 1996. *Climate Change and the Financial Sector–The Emerging Threat, the Solar Solution.* Munich: Gerling Akademie Verlag.

Lipson, Charles. 1985. *Standing Guard: Protecting Foreign Capital in the Nine-*

teenth and Twentieth Centuries. Berkeley and Los Angeles: University of California Press.

Marine Stewardship Council. 2000. "Fishery Stakeholders Endorse MSC." Available from <www.panda.org/endangeredseas/msc/vol3news/page1.htm>.

Mathews, Jessica T. 1997. "Power Shift." *Foreign Affairs,* vol. 76, no. 1, pp. 50–66.

Mazur, Jay. 2000. "Labour's New Internationalism." *Foreign Affairs* (January–February).

Millstein, Ira M., and Business Sector Advisory Group on Corporate Governance. 1998. "Corporate Governance: Improving Competitiveness and Access to Capital in Global Markets: A Report to the OECD." Paris: Organization for Economic Cooperation and Development.

Mitchell, John. 1998. "Editor's Overview," in *Companies in a World of Conflict,* ed. John Mitchell. London: Royal Institute of International Affairs and Earthscan Publications.

Mokhiber, Russell, and Robert Weissman. 1999. *Corporate Predators: The Hunt for Mega-Profits and the Attack on Democracy.* Monroe, Maine: Common Courage.

Moon, Peter, and Raj Thamotheram. 2000. "Corporations Become 'Socially Responsible.'" *The Independent,* December 12.

Moore, Curtis, and Alan Miller. 1994. *Green Gold: Japan, Germany and the United States, and the Race for Environmental Technology.* Boston: Beacon Press.

Moran, Theodore. 1999. *Foreign Direct Investment and Development: The New Policy Agenda for Developing Countries and Economies in Transition.* Washington, D.C.: Institute for International Economics.

MORI. 1999. "Millennium Poll." Press Release, September 30. Available at <www.mori.com>.

Morrin, Douglas S. 2000. "People Before Profits: Pursuing Corporate Accountability for Labor Rights Violations Abroad Through the Alien Tort Claims Act." *Boston College Third World Law Journal,* vol. 20, no. 2.

Murphy, David F., and Jem Bendell. 1997. *In the Company of Partners: Business, Environmental Groups, and Sustainable Development Post-Rio.* Bristol, U.K.: The Policy Press.

Nelson, Jane. 1996. *Business as Partners in Development: Creating Wealth for Countries, Companies and Communities.* London: Prince of Wales Business Leaders Forum.

Nelson, Jane, and Simon Zadek. n.d. *Partnership Alchemy: New Social Partnerships in Europe.* Copenhagen: Copenhagen Centre.

OECD. 1998. "Codes of Corporate Conduct." Trade Directorate Trade Committee. Paris: OECD.

Ohmae, Kenichi. 1995. *The End of the Nation State: The Rise of Regional Economies.* New York: The Free Press.

Olson, Mancur. 1965. *The Logic of Collective Action: Public Goods and the Theory of Groups.* Cambridge, Mass.: Harvard University Press.

Oman, Charles. 1984. *New Forms of Investment in Developing Countries.* Paris: OECD.

Online Privacy Alliance (OPA). 1999. "OPA Report on the Top 100, Executive Summary." Washington, D.C.: OPA.

Opinion Leader Research. 2000. *Does the City Have a Social Conscience?* London: Control Risks Group.

Oxford Analytica and Prince of Wales Business Leaders Forum. 2000. *Changing Corporate Roles and Responsibilities: Business and Socially Responsible Investment.* London: Oxford Analytica and Prince of Wales Business Leaders Forum.

Pinkham, Douglas G. 2000. "Activist Groups Use the Net to Gain Power and Influence." Press Release, Foundation for Public Affairs, Washington, D.C.

Porter, Gareth, and Janet Welsh Brown. 1996. *Global Environmental Politics.* Boulder, Colo.: Westview Press.

Prakash, Aseem. 2000. *Greening the Firm: The Politics of Corporate Environmentalism.* Cambridge, U.K.: Cambridge University Press.

Prakash, Aseem, and Jeffrey A. Hart, eds. 1999. *Globalization and Governance.* Routledge/RIPE Studies in Global Political Economy. London and New York: Routledge.

Privacy Journal. 2000. "Policy Models." Available at <www.townonline.com/specials/privacy>.

Rauch, Jonathan. 2000. "The New Old Economy: Oil, Computers, and the Reinvention of the Earth." *Atlantic Monthly,* vol. 287, no. 1, pp. 35–49.

Reinicke, Wolfgang. 1997. "Global Public Policy." *Foreign Affairs* (November–December), pp. 127–55.

Riverside Publishing Company. 1984. *Webster's II New Riverside University Dictionary.* Boston: Houghton Mifflin.

Rodrik, Dani. 1997. *Has Globalization Gone Too Far?* Washington, D.C.: Institute for International Economics.

Royal Dutch/Shell. 2000. *How Do We Stand? People, Planet, and Profits, The Shell Report 2000.* London: Royal Dutch/Shell.

Ruggie, John Gerard. 1983. "International Regimes, Transactions, and Change: Embedded Liberalism in the Postwar Economic Order." In *International Regimes,* ed. Stephen Krasner. Ithaca, N.Y.: Cornell University Press, pp. 195–231.

Schreurs, Miranda, and Elizabeth Economy, eds. 1997. *The Internationalization of Environmental Protection.* Cambridge, U.K.: Cambridge University Press.

Schwartz, Peter, and Blair Gibb. 1999. *When Good Companies Do Bad Things.* New York: John Wiley & Sons.

Shailor, Barbara. 1998. "Workers' Rights: The Human Rights Struggle of Our Time." *Focus: Public Services International*, no. 3, pp. 24–9.

Simmons, P. J. 1998. "Learning to Live with NGOs." *Foreign Policy*, no. 112, pp. 82–96.

Smith, Mark A. 2000. *American Business and Political Power: Public Opinion, Elections, and Democracy*. Chicago: University of Chicago Press.

Social Investment Forum. 2000. *SIF Research: 1999 Trends Report*. Available at <www.socialinvest.org/Areas/research/trends/1999-Trends.htm>.

Spar, Debora L. 1998. "The Spotlight and the Bottom Line: How Multinationals Export Human Rights." *Foreign Affairs*, vol. 77, no. 2:, pp. 7–12.

Spar, Debora, and Jeffrey Busgang. 1996. "Ruling the Net." *Harvard Business Review* vol. 74, no. 3, p. 125.

Steer, David. 1999. "Privacy Practices Help Build Trust, Get and Retain Web Customers." *ECmgt.com*, vol. 1, no. 10.

Stopford, John M., Susan Strange, with John S. Henley. 1991. *Rival States, Rival Firms: Competition for World Market Shares*. New York: Cambridge University Press.

Strange, Susan. 1996. *The Retreat of the State: The Diffusion of Power in the World Economy*. New York: Cambridge University Press.

Swire, Peter P., and Robert E. Litan. 1998. *None of Your Business: World Data Flows, Electronic Commerce, and the European Privacy Directive*. Washington, D.C.: Brookings Institution Press.

The Natural Step (TNS). 2000. "What Is the Natural Step?" Available at <www.naturalstep.org/what/index_what.html>.

Thomson, Stephen. 2000. *Investment Patterns in a Longer-Term Perspective*. Paris: OECD.

Trans-Atlantic Consumer Dialogue (TACD). 1999. *Recommendations on Electronic Commerce*. Brussels: TACD.

TRUSTe (2000a). *How Does Privacy Impact Your Bottom Line?* Available at <http:// www.truste.org/webpublishers/pub_bottom.html>.

———. 2000b. *TRUSTe and RealNetworks Collaborate to Close Privacy Gap*. Available at <www.truste.org/about/about_software.html>.

U.K. Data Protection Registrar. 1999. "The Eighth Data Protection Principle and Transborder Dataflows: Preliminary Views." London: UK Data Protection Registrar.

UN Conference on Environment and Development (UNCED). 1992. *Agenda 21 Earth Summit: United Nations Program of Action from Rio*. New York: United Nations Publications.

UNCTAD. 2000. *World Investment Report*. Geneva: UNCTAD.

UNCTAD. 1998. *World Investment Report: Trends and Determinants*. Geneva: UNCTAD.

UNEP and SustainAbility. 1997. *Benchmark Survey: Corporate Environmental Reporting*. Nairobi and New York: UNEP.

U.S. Bureau of Labor Statistics. 1998. "International Comparisons of Hourly Compensation Costs for Production Workers in Manufacturing, 1975–1997." Washington, D.C.: U.S. Department of Labor, Bureau of Labor Statistics.

———. 1999. "International Comparisons of Hourly Compensation Costs for Production Workers in Manufacturing, 1999." Washington, D.C.: U.S. Department of Labor, Bureau of Labor Statistics.

U.S. White House. 1999. *Framework for Global Electronic Commerce.* Washington, D.C.: White House.

Varley, Pamela, ed. 1998. *The Sweatshop Quandary: Corporate Responsibility on the Global Frontier.* Washington, D.C.: Investor Responsibility Research Center.

Vogel, Steven. 1996. *Freer Markets, More Rules: Regulatory Reform in Advanced Industrial Countries.* Ithaca, N.Y.: Cornell University Press.

Wapner, Kevin Paul. 1996. *Environmental Activism and World Civic Politics.* Albany, N.Y.: State University of New York.

Welte, Jim. 2000. "Five Questions with . . . Esther Dyson, Chairman of EdVentures Holdings." *Business 2.0* (December 1). Available at <www.business2.com/content/ channels/ebusiness/2000/12/01/23230>.

Wilkinson, Rorden, and Steve Hughes. 2000. "Labor Standards and Global Governance: Examining the Dimensions of Institutional Engagement." *Global Governance*, vol. 6, no. 2, pp. 259–77.

Williamson, Jeffrey G. 1997. "Globalization and Inequality: Past and Present." The *World Bank Research Observer*, vol. 12, no. 2, p. 117.

Williamson, Oliver. 1985. *The Economic Institutions of Capitalism: Firms, Markets, Relational Contracting.* State College, Penn.: Pennsylvania University Press.

Wise, Carol, ed. 1998. *The Post-NAFTA Political Economy: Mexico and the Western World.* State College, Penn.: Pennsylvania University Press.

World Bank. 1997. *World Development Report 1997.* New York: Oxford University Press.

———. 1998. *1998 World Development Indicators.* Washington, D.C.: World Bank.

Yosie, Terry, and Tim Herbst. 1998. *The Journey Toward Corporate Environmental Excellence.* Washington, D.C.: Enterprise for the Environment.

Zuckerman, Amy. 1998a. "Global Standards Can Be a Drag on the Bottom Line." *Journal of Commerce*, July 7, p. 1.

———. 1998b. "Many Stunned by Social Accountability Standard from Little-Known Organization." *Journal of Commerce*, April 8, p. 14.

Index

About the Author

VIRGINIA HAUFLER directed the project on the Role of the Private Sector in International Affairs at the Carnegie Endowment for International Peace from 1998–99. She is an associate professor at the University of Maryland, College Park, and has served as consultant to the U.S. Department of State, the Office of the Secretary-General of the United Nations, the International Labor Organization, and others. She is the author of *Dangerous Commerce: Insurance and the Management of International Risk* (Cornell University Press, 1997), and co-editor with A. Claire Cutler and Tony Porter of *Private Authority and International Affairs* (State University of New York Press, 1999). Dr. Haufler has written extensively on various aspects of business–government relations, global governance, and international political economy. She earned her M.A./Ph.D. in government from Cornell University in 1991 and her B.A. in international affairs from Pennsylvania State University in 1979.

Carnegie Endowment for International Peace

THE CARNEGIE ENDOWMENT is a private, nonprofit organization dedicated to advancing cooperation between nations and promoting active international engagement by the United States. Founded in 1910, its work is nonpartisan and dedicated to achieving practical results. Through research, publishing, convening and, on occasion, creating new institutions and international networks, Endowment associates shape fresh policy approaches. Their interests span geographic regions and the relations between governments, business, international organizations, and civil society, focusing on the economic, political, and technological forces driving global change. Through its Carnegie Moscow Center, the Endowment helps to develop a tradition of public policy analysis in the states of the former Soviet Union and to improve relations between Russia and the United States. The Endowment publishes *Foreign Policy*, one of the world's leading magazines of international politics and economics, which reaches readers in more than 120 countries and in several languages.